understanding your baby

A parent's guide to progress in the first year and beyond

Kyra Karmiloff, MSc &
Dr. Annette Karmiloff-Smith, PhD

hamlyn

An Hachette UK company
www.hachette.co.uk

First published in Great Britain in 2010 by
Carroll & Brown Publishers Limited

This edition published in 2015 by Hamlyn,
a division of Octopus Publishing Group Ltd
Carmelite House, 50 Victoria Embankment,
London EC4Y 0DZ
www.octopusbooks.co.uk
www.octopusbooksusa.com

Distributed in the US by Hachette Book Group
1290 Avenue of the Americas, 4th and 5th Floors
New York, NY 10020

Distributed in Canada by Canadian Manda Group
664 Annette St., Toronto, Ontario, Canada M6S 2C8

ISBN 978-0-600-63164-4

Printed and bound in China

2 4 6 8 10 9 7 5 3 1

Deputy Art Director: Yasia Williams-Leedham
Senior Editor: Leanne Bryan
Assistant Production Manager: Caroline Alberti
Photography: Jules Selmes

Contents

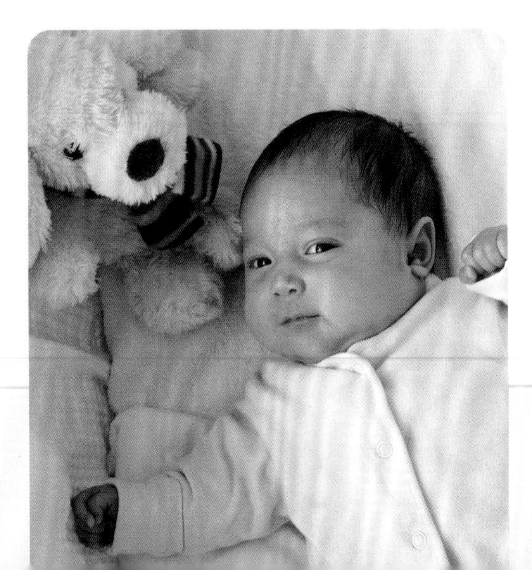

3 How your baby learns to communicate

4 How your baby learns to move

How your baby learns to think

Welcome to your baby's world

Your infant arrived in the world already equipped with many reflexes and instincts that will help him to explore and adapt to his physical environment as well as find his place in the social world. Our aim is to help you to see the world through your baby's eyes so that you will be better equipped to assist him on his journey of discovery.

The book covers the first three years of life and looks at all the developmental steps your new baby will take on his way to becoming a walking, talking, mischievous toddler. In the five chapters that follow, you will get an insight into how your baby finds out about himself and his physical and social environments through interaction, experience, trial and error, and nurturing.

Each chapter deals with a different aspect of your baby's life from birth to toddlerhood. Throughout the book, you will find helpful tips and suggestions about how you, the parent, can make learning a joy and positively influence your child's journey toward independence.

The first chapter looks at infant behavior with the aim of helping you to understand all the exciting things happening to your baby as he adapts to life outside the womb. The second chapter examines your baby's early experiences

of his social world and family life, looking at how he responds to others and starts forming a sense of self. This is followed by a chapter on how your baby learns to understand and produce language.

In the fourth chapter, the focus is on the physical world, looking at your baby's gross and fine motor development, from learning to reach and manipulate objects to becoming mobile.

Finally, chapter five examines your baby's developing intelligence by looking at your child's sensory experiences and amazing learning, memory, and problem-solving skills.

Like all parents, you will eagerly await each new development, but do remember that every child is unique and will develop at his own pace. Our book aims to provide you with a general idea of developmental steps, and as long as your baby seems to be progressing well, do not focus on specific ages. However, if you are worried that your child is lagging behind other babies of a similar age, do not hesitate to talk to your family physician or healthcare provider, who can examine your child and, if necessary, arrange for assessment by a specialist to make sure everything is okay.

1

Your baby's first weeks in the outside world

UNDERSTANDING EARLY INFANT BEHAVIOR

Being able to make sense of your newborn's behavior can go a long way toward helping you adjust to life with your new baby. As a starting point, the best advice we can give is for you to try to see the world through your little one's eyes so that you can appreciate how he makes sense of his environment. Understanding what his senses "tell" him, for example, will help you to decode some of his responses and anticipate his needs.

After the dark comfort and warmth of the womb, the outside world is a bewildering place for your little one. Although fetuses open and close their eyes, there is nothing much to look at in the womb. At birth, however, as soon as your baby opened his eyes—usually the instant he started to breathe—he was bombarded with faces, objects, and shapes, all of them new and interesting but confusing, too.

This new world is also a noisy place for your newborn, who was used to the muffling effect of amniotic fluid and the gentle rhythms of your heartbeat and blood flow.

However, it isn't just his eyes and ears that help your baby to explore and get accustomed to life in the outside world. His senses of smell and touch are also important.

What your baby can see

During the first few weeks of life, your baby's visual acuity is only sharp enough to focus 8–10 inches away, which is approximately the distance that separates a baby's face from his mother's as he feeds. Therefore, much of your

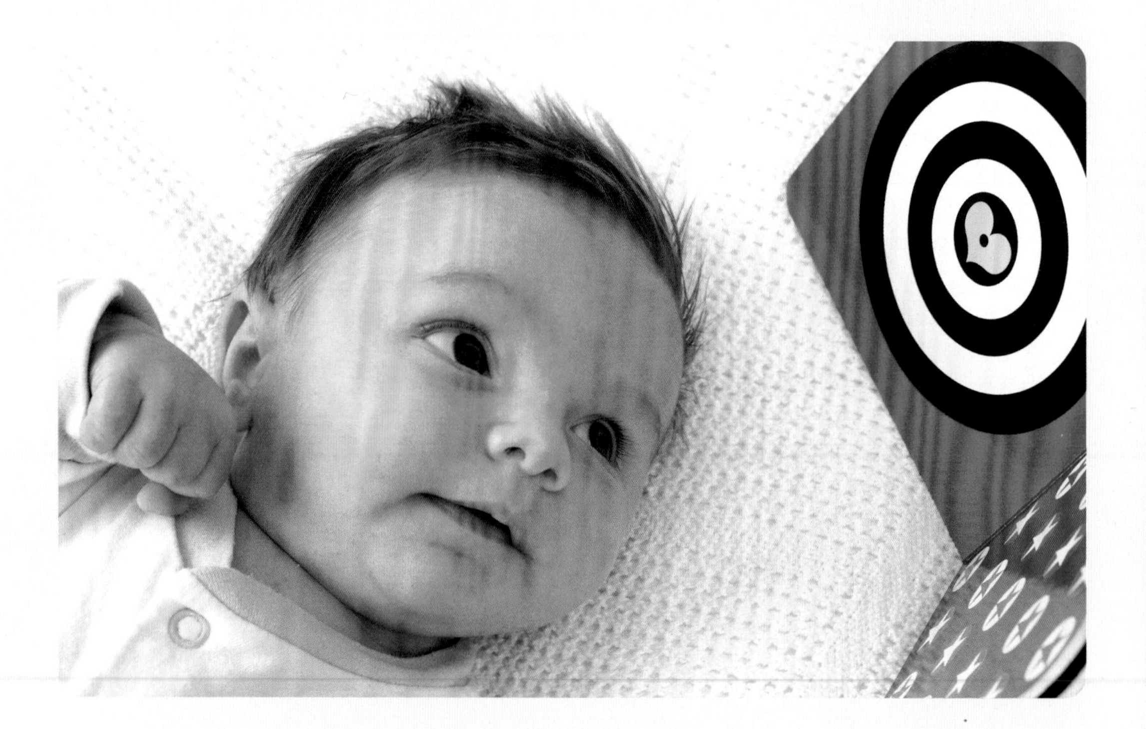

little one's world looks blurry and indistinct during the first month or two. For this reason, your newborn, like other young infants, prefers to focus most of his attention on faces, especially those of you and your partner and any siblings.

At first, details such as facial features are hard to make out. However, young babies are resourceful creatures; your baby will learn to recognize family members by memorizing other characteristics, such as facial contours, hairstyles, voices, and smells (see below). So this is definitely not the time for mom or dad to get a new hairstyle.

In terms of visual stimulation, apart from faces, it is movement in which your young infant is most interested. You may have noticed your little one becoming suddenly distracted while feeding, for example, by an object or person crossing his field of vision. At this early stage, he has yet to gain proper control over his eyes, so his ability to track the object smoothly is limited. He will, nevertheless, give it his best shot by turning his head and attempting to follow the movement with his eyes. You can help him develop visual tracking (see the box, page 96) and it won't be long before your baby progresses from jerky eye movements to smoother tracking. This will enable him, after a few weeks, to anticipate the object's trajectory enough to attempt swiping, and eventually reaching and grasping.

What your baby can hear

Sounds, too, provide your infant with constant stimulation and are an important part of learning to communicate later on. For this reason, all newborns are given a hearing assessment to be sure there are no problems (see the box, page 134). During the first weeks of life, your baby will prefer to concentrate most of his listening attention on voices, his mother's in particular. This is because mom's voice is already a familiar sound. Although the womb acts as a filter for sounds and voices in the outside world, an unborn baby is able to hear enough of his mother's unique voice to recognize it instantly at birth. It is the most soothing and comforting sound a newborn can hear, which is why talking or singing to your baby often has an instantly calming effect. Other voices, too, will be a big draw to your infant, and family members and carers should be encouraged to talk to him as often as possible. At this early stage, your baby has little control over his own voice, and may surprise himself with the grunts, gurgles, sighs, and other sounds he makes. As he gets to grips with his own voice and learns to manipulate it to catch your attention, you will notice attempts at increasingly diverse sounds. He may begin to cry out in different ways to communicate his needs; he will coo and blow raspberries to prompt smiles and interaction, and he will start practicing language sounds in preparation for babbling.

The importance of smell and touch

Smell is extremely well-developed at birth—perhaps to make up for blurry vision—and is used by your infant to help locate familiar people and food sources. Your newborn will quickly learn to differentiate between individual smells and can be soothed by the ones linked to comfort and care. That's why you shouldn't mask your natural smell with artificial scents; they are not pleasant for his tiny nose and may cause some confusion.

By now, you are familiar with the rooting reflex that makes your baby turn his head in response to a stroke on the cheek, but look closer and you will see that even in the absence of sound or touch, he may turn in your direction, after recognizing your familiar odor. This is one of the reasons why moms and dads are encouraged to make skin-to-skin contact with their newborns as often as possible. This type of closeness not only provides comfort to your baby, it also promotes the development of touch and smell, helping your infant to learn more about his parents, and to form a strong and close bond with you.

Memories from the womb

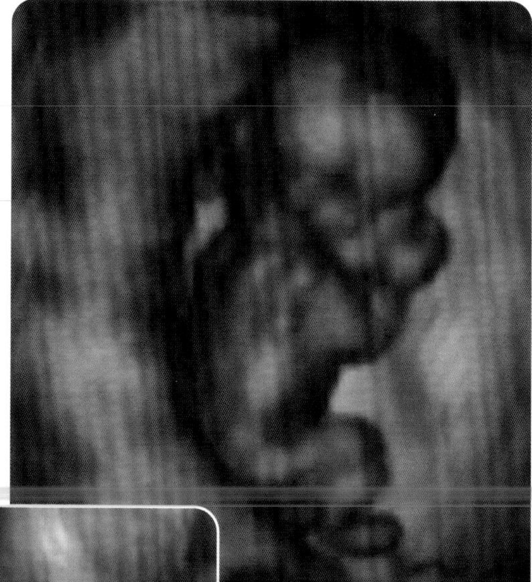

Prenatal experiences play an important role in the transition from the uterus to the outside world. Your baby was born with an invaluable store of knowledge—a selection of memories from life inside the uterus—that enables him to recognize, distinguish, and show preference for important aspects of his new environment, such as his mother's voice, the sound patterns of his mother tongue, and the taste of mother's milk.

By the time your unborn baby reached six months gestation, his taste buds had already developed, and he was able to tell whether the amniotic liquid tasted bitter, sweet, or sour. This marked the beginning of his taste preferences. It is thought that by becoming familiar with flavors most often present in his mother's diet, a baby prepares himself for the unique taste of his mother's milk. Indeed, mothers who change their diets dramatically once their babies are born can have difficulty getting their infants to accept their breast milk. So this is definitely not the time to develop new food habits. If your baby had not been exposed to strong flavors in the womb, he will not appreciate mommy's milk suddenly taking on the tang of spicy food!

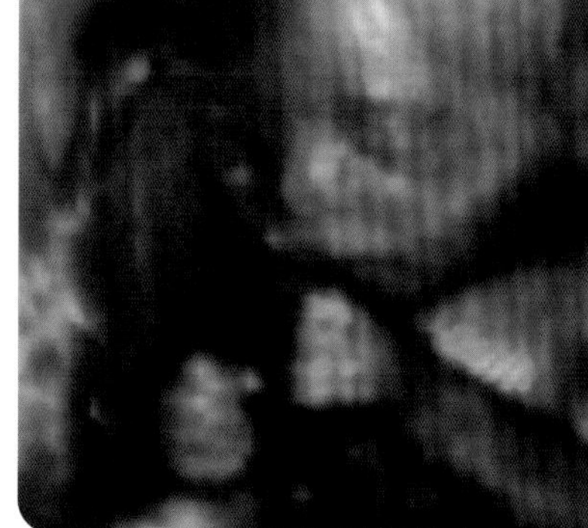

Memories for sound are also noticeable in a newly born infant. The human sense of hearing develops as early as fifteen to twenty weeks gestation. By twenty-five weeks, ultrasound images show that fetuses actually react to what they are hearing with startle responses if the noise is sudden. Sounds penetrating the womb can cause the heartbeat and levels of leg activity to increase, and if they have a distinct rhythm, such as music, a fetus might even begin to perform repetitive movements—a little dancer in the making.

As a result of all this prenatal stimulation and experience, only moments after birth your baby can already demonstrate preferences for his mother's voice, the taste of her milk, and even for pieces of music played regularly during the final months of pregnancy. This explains why repeating the experiences after he is born can have an immediately calming effect on your fractious newborn.

The next time you are struggling to calm your infant, try to imagine what life was like for him in the womb and look for ways to re-create the same kind of calm and comfort.

Newborn reflexes

Reflexes are bodily reactions that occur automatically without a person's intention or will. As adults, we pay little attention to them but, for the human newborn, they play an important survival role. Reflexes are responsible for many of your infant's early movements and responses. A doctor will check all of a baby's natural reflexes just after birth.

In the fluid-filled world of the womb, your baby's every need was monitored and met. In the outside world—where food, warmth, safety, and comfort come intermittently and sometimes only by request—surviving is far more difficult. Luckily, thanks to evolution and the clever designs of nature, your baby arrived in the world equipped with certain automatic functions that help his body cope with the demands of his new environment and help to ensure that he receives all the care he needs.

There are many recognized newborn reflexes. Some are there to help your baby's body cope with the outside world, others act as precursors to later voluntary responses, and still others appear to be redundant leftovers of intrauterine development with no apparent purpose for life in the outside world. Here, we will concentrate on the most noticeable ones, as well as those that seem to contribute positively to your baby's development. Before looking at those, however, let's look at breathing.

The breathing reflex

Not commonly listed as one of the main newborn reflexes, breathing is one of the first to come into play at birth. We, of course, take breathing for granted, but for the tiny newborn, it is another hurdle to overcome. Infant lungs—even those of full-term babies—are not well developed at birth. They contain far fewer alveoli than adult lungs (less than 15 percent), which means that an infant's capacity to take in oxygen is considerably reduced. Breathing remains tenuous for the first two years of life, which is why some babies may be at higher risk of respiratory problems.

Other survival reflexes

Unlike the offspring of certain other species, who are up and running moments after birth, human infants arrive in the world completely dependent. Your baby is totally dependent on you to feed, protect, and comfort him, and to keep him warm. Nevertheless, evolution has supplied him with a few reflexes useful for life outside the uterus, including the rooting, sucking, and swallowing reflexes that prompt your baby to turn toward a milk source, latch on, and take in food. Like most automatic behaviors, however, even feeding necessitates a degree of learning. It is a skill that may be precipitated by reflexes but still requires honing to perfection by trial and error and a lot of practice.

Other useful reflexes are the pupillary and blink reflexes that cause pupils to constrict and

The rooting reflex *makes your baby turn to your breast to seek nourishment. It can be elicited by stroking the side of his cheek with your finger.*

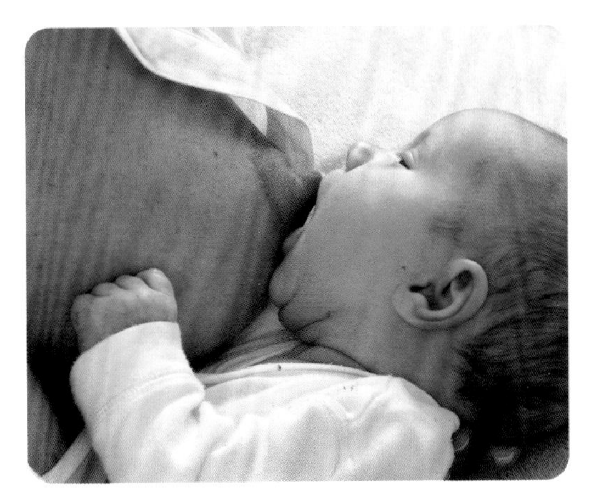

eyelids to close in response to bright lights, thereby protecting the eyes. There is also the Moro, or startle, reflex, by which sudden noises or sensations prompt your infant to react by splaying out his limbs and becoming more aroused. This reflex alerts your baby to a potential nearby danger.

Some reflexes are temporary

Reflexes, such as the startle reflex, the grasping, or palmar, reflex (see page 15), and the stepping reflex (see page 88), fade soon after birth and seem unconnected to the immediate needs of infant survival. Human babies, unlike other primates, don't need to hang onto their mothers. Bipedalism (walking upright on two legs) means that a human mother's hands are free to hold her infant, leaving the infant's hands idle. So why did this reflex survive evolution? It may well be that in humans the original function of the grasping reflex has now been replaced by a need for early tactile exploration of the world. In the uterus, for example, a fetus will grasp the umbilical cord whenever it brushes against his hand, thereby stimulating his sense of touch. Similar experiences, both in the womb and in the outside world, encourage tactile learning and development. This may be why this reflex still exists and remains strong in the first few months after birth.

The stepping reflex will disappear as your baby's limbs lengthen and get heavier and he

WATER BABY

At birth, your little one is still possessed of certain clever body mechanisms, designed for life in the womb, which do not function in later life. For instance, during a limited period, your newborn can swim underwater without filling his lungs. This is because his voice box has yet to descend. Before this happens, a valve will automatically shut off the passage between his mouth and lungs.

Within weeks of birth this mechanism, along with other reflexes not particularly useful to life in the outside world, will disappear and he will no longer be automatically protected from breathing in water. It is all part of the body's adaptation to its new environment.

It is a good idea to get your baby used to water early. As soon as you get the "all clear" from your healthcare provider (normally after your baby has received the appropriate immunizations), try to enroll in parent-and-baby swimming lessons. These are often available for babies from six months old, and you will be able to learn under supervision how to make the most of your baby's aquatic skills. You could also enjoy sharing baths together at home, but remember to adjust the temperature to your little one's needs—and have another adult on hand, if possible, because wet babies are slippery and get cold fast and it can be awkward for the two of you to exit the bath at once.

If you place your finger against your infant's palm, he will automatically tighten his fingers around it. The origins of this reflex are apparent in the behavior of newborn primates, our ancestral cousins. From the moment they are born, baby monkeys and apes depend on their ability to hold tightly onto their mothers' bodies as they move around. Without this, mothers and babies would become separated.

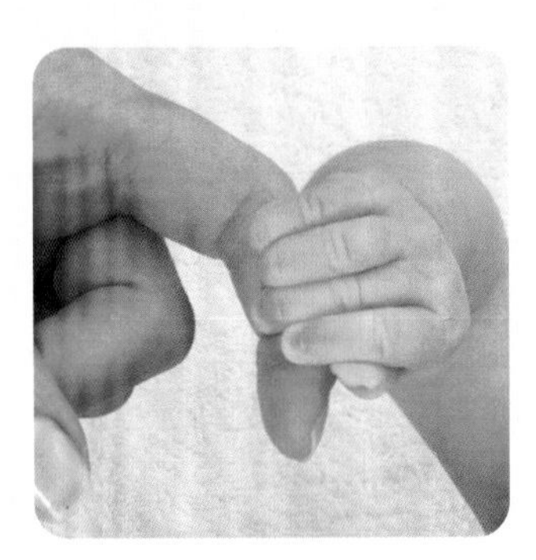

gains control over his body. Although it may seem unconnected to the process of learning to walk—which occurs a year later—in fact, practicing the reflex early on may set up a template for walking in the memory stores of the brain. As the stepping action is repeated in sequences, links are formed between the cells and circuits in the areas of your baby's brain responsible for walking. When he is strong enough to support his own weight, this template may be called upon and strengthened to help with the practice and learning processes involved in walking.

Assessing a baby's reflexes

Because they are automatic and present across all human infants, doctors check all of these reflexes at birth and again a few weeks later to assess a newborn's health and development. The lack of strong reflexes may indicate ill-health or developmental problems that could have occurred either in the uterus or during birth. However, do not worry if your baby does not respond as expected, because reflexes can be affected by many factors, such as your baby's level of alertness, his general well-being at the time, the room temperature, and noise levels.

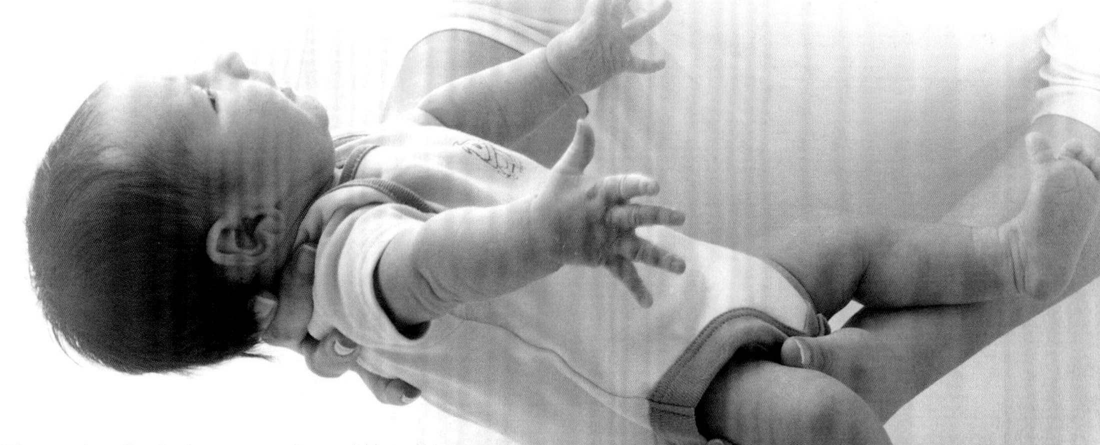

The startle reflex *involves your newborn quickly moving his arms upward and outward until they are straight at the elbow in response to a sudden noise, vibration, or movement.*

Learning to sleep and sleeping to learn

Paradoxically, the main "activity" of a newborn's life is sleep. In the first few weeks of life, your infant will spend up to two-thirds of his time asleep. Sleep is vital to your baby's overall healthy development and is crucial for learning. Without sleep, his brain would struggle to reorganize all the information he takes in during the day when he is awake and to consolidate it in long-term memory.

During his early months, every waking minute is filled with new experiences—smells, sounds, sights, and sensations. His infant brain does its best to cope with all this information with the help of short-term memory, but it is at night, when your baby's eyes and ears are at rest, that this information is processed. While your little one sleeps, his brain remains busy. In fact, some parts of his brain are more active during sleep than during wakefulness. They sift through the experiences of the day to create richer mental images in long-term memory—a crucial part of the learning process.

Sleep is also the time during which your baby's body releases most of its growth hormones. Because he has to double his weight over the next few months, the more sleep he gets, the better.

A learned skill

Your baby, however, did not come into the world equipped with the ability to sleep through the night. During the early months, his tiny stomach can only take in enough food to last a few hours, so he needs to wake regularly to replenish his stocks. However, this isn't the only reason your little one wakes so often. At this

stage, he does not know the difference between day and night, nor can he smoothly pass between the different sleep phases. Sleeping is not something that comes as naturally as we assume. It is a skill that requires a certain amount of learning. The ability to self-soothe and fall asleep alone, and to remain peacefully asleep as the brain progresses from active sleep to deep sleep, can take months of practice.

Sleeping is somewhat of a roller-coaster experience. As you fall asleep, your adult brain passes through four phases of deepening rest, then rises back through the stages to a period of REM (rapid eye movement) sleep, when you dream and brain activity is high. Over an eight-hour period of rest, your brain will go through this cycle four or five times. For adults, the process is relatively smooth and most of us remain blissfully unaware of what is going on as we sleep the night away. On the occasions that you do wake up and see that it is still night, you are able to shut your eyes, clear your mind, and return to sleep.

However, time is not clearly divided between night and day for your little one. Although his sleeping cycle at this stage involves fewer phases—babies progress directly from active/REM sleep to deep sleep—he may stir, open his eyes, or even cry out as he passes from one sleep state to another. If he awakens, for whatever reason, at any stage during the night, he will not have the instinct to know that now is not the right time to be awake, nor does he yet possess the skills needed to calm himself down and fall back to sleep. At this stage, he still needs some reassurance and practice to learn how to cope with waking up alone during the night.

Helping your baby to sleep

There are several things that you can do to help your baby sleep more peacefully and learn about night and day. Taking a different approach to daylight feeds as opposed to night ones is a good first step.

During the day

Use feeding time as an opportunity to bond with your infant. Encourage plenty of eye contact and talk to your little one as he feeds.

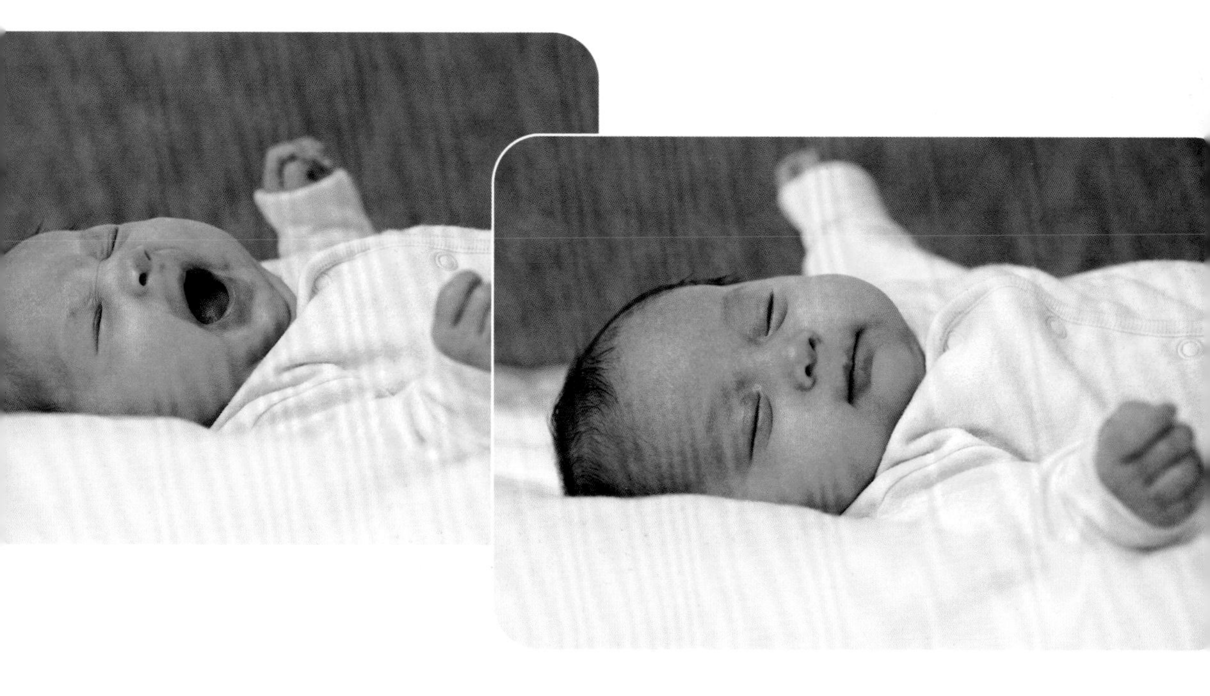

Also, keep the curtains open or the lights on. When you put him into his crib for naps, don't insist on total darkness and complete silence—he needs to learn to fall asleep in different conditions. Always try to put him into bed while awake or at least partly awake, so that he begins to get used to the idea of going to sleep on his own. Babies have good memories, so if you rock your baby to sleep in your arms, he'll not only expect to still be there when he wakes up, but will quickly get used to relying on this as a method of soothing. Another reason to put him into his crib to sleep while he is still awake is that it will help him to associate sleeping and waking up with being safe and calm in his crib.

When your baby wakes at night

Resist the temptation to jump out of bed at your baby's every cry or movement—you may be interrupting a stage of semisleep when he is working his way through one sleep state to another. Wait a few minutes and make sure that he is really awake and in need of attention before going to him. If a night feed is needed, pick him up but stay quiet and avoid eye contact and any talk. Keep lighting and fuss to a minimum, even if a diaper change is necessary. Your aim should be to make the sleep interruption as short and calm as possible to mark clearly the difference between night and day. This will help your baby develop a better diurnal rhythm, or day–night cycle, which will eventually lead to him going to sleep more easily by himself and staying asleep for longer stretches at night.

HOW *you can help*

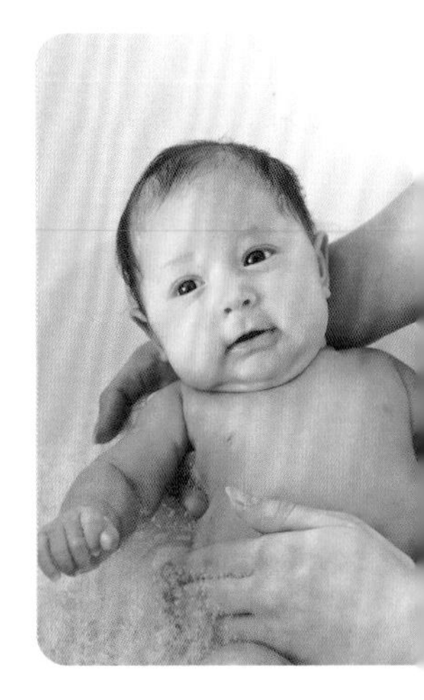

It is never too early to start good bedtime habits. While it is tempting to resort to tried-and-tested methods whenever your baby gets fractious—rocking or patting or the motion of a car ride or stroller—as often as possible, put him into his crib for naps while he is still partly awake. This is good training for sleeping through the night, because it teaches your infant to cope with self-soothing and falling asleep alone.

To help him along, work up to each sleep period with a fixed routine—

particularly in the evening when you are getting him ready for bed for the night.

Start with a bath, some quiet time listening to music or singing to him in the semidark, or reading a story. When you give him the last feed of the day, this should be done as calmly and silently as possible. Encourage him to remain awake but relaxed, then lie him down, soothe him a little, if necessary, but don't engage in eye contact or interaction, and leave the room. Above all, once the sleep routine has begun, avoid excitement and stimulation—save the fun for the morning. This is quiet time.

If your baby dozes through much of the day or regularly falls asleep as he feeds, try to actively keep him awake for increasing periods and during all of his feeds. Only you can teach him that his longest sleep should happen at night.

Start to fit his routines into the family ones, reorganizing his naps so that the last one of the day is not too close to bedtime.

Especially young babies are often fractious and unsettled in the evenings before going to bed. They seem to need to have a feeding and crying frenzy before settling for the night; this can be hard for you, because you may be tired at the end of the day, too. Don't worry; crying is good for the lungs, and at this stage his eating habits will be far from settled. This difficult phase only lasts a few weeks, and with patience and practice and a good daily routine, you will find that life soon settles into a regular pattern out of which will come increasingly peaceful nights.

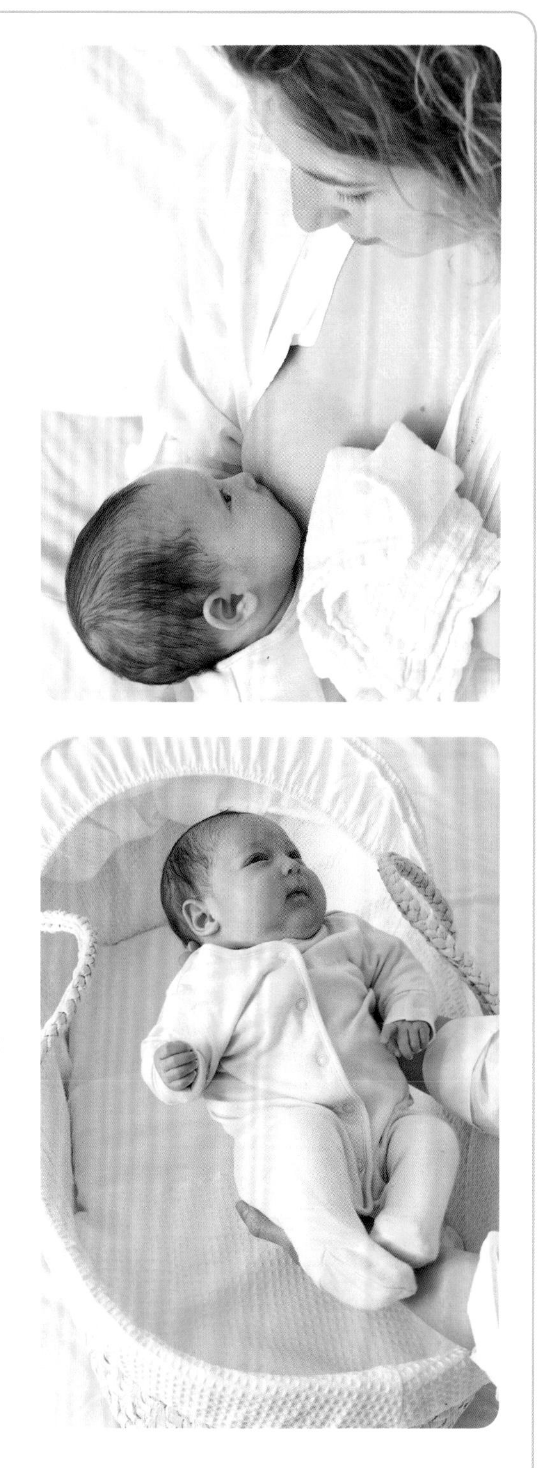

2

How your baby becomes a social being

COMPREHENDING SELF AND OTHERS

How do infants come to understand that they are individuals, with bodies, minds, ideas, and emotions of their own, who exist alongside other individuals who are all members of a wider social world? The answer lies in a combination of processes that start in infancy, develop through childhood, and continue long into adulthood. These involve getting to know oneself, becoming aware of others, and forming relationships—first within the family unit, then beyond it to include an increasingly diverse social group.

Exploring her body parts *is both fun for your baby and a way to develop a sense of self.*

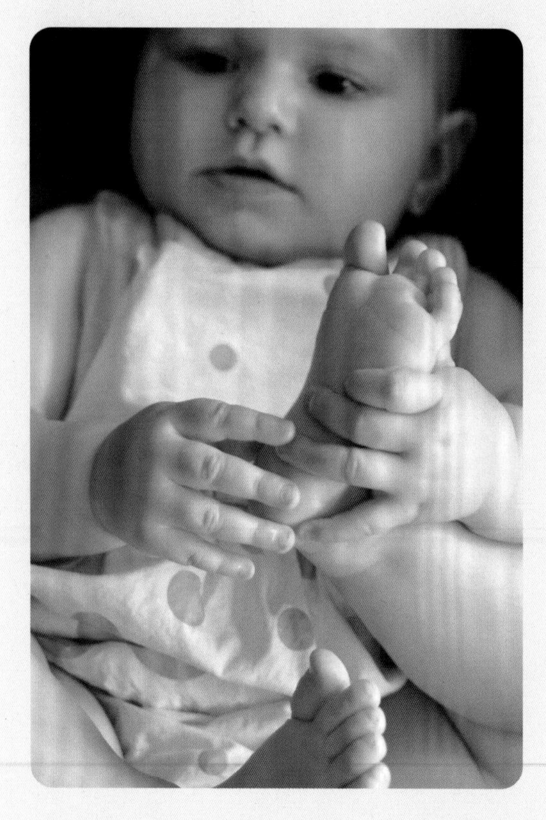

Developing self-awareness

This is a lengthy process that starts with the simple discovery by an infant that she can control her body parts. At around two months of age, and after weeks of awkward, jerky kicking and flaying of arms, your baby starts to make more purposeful movements, grabbing and playing with her own hands, holding onto her feet, swiping at objects, and generally gaining better control over her head, limbs, facial expressions, and vocalizations. Her new enthusiasm for putting everything in her mouth has nothing to do with hunger; instead, it reveals a growing appetite for knowledge. The nerve endings in her mouth are initially more sensitive than those in her fingers, so her mouth offers the perfect means for exploring objects.

Becoming self-aware and learning to be an individual member of the social world also involves learning about gender. It doesn't matter how many dolls you buy your baby son, or trains you offer to your baby daughter, your child will probably turn out to be as conventional as others, at least during her early years. Gender-related play occurs in almost all children, not only as a result of peer pressure in playgroups, but also from subtle clues you yourself unwittingly give your child.

Without meaning to, adults behave differently toward baby boys and girls in the way we hold, speak to, and treat them. Your infant will pick up on these subtle signs and construct her own identity accordingly.

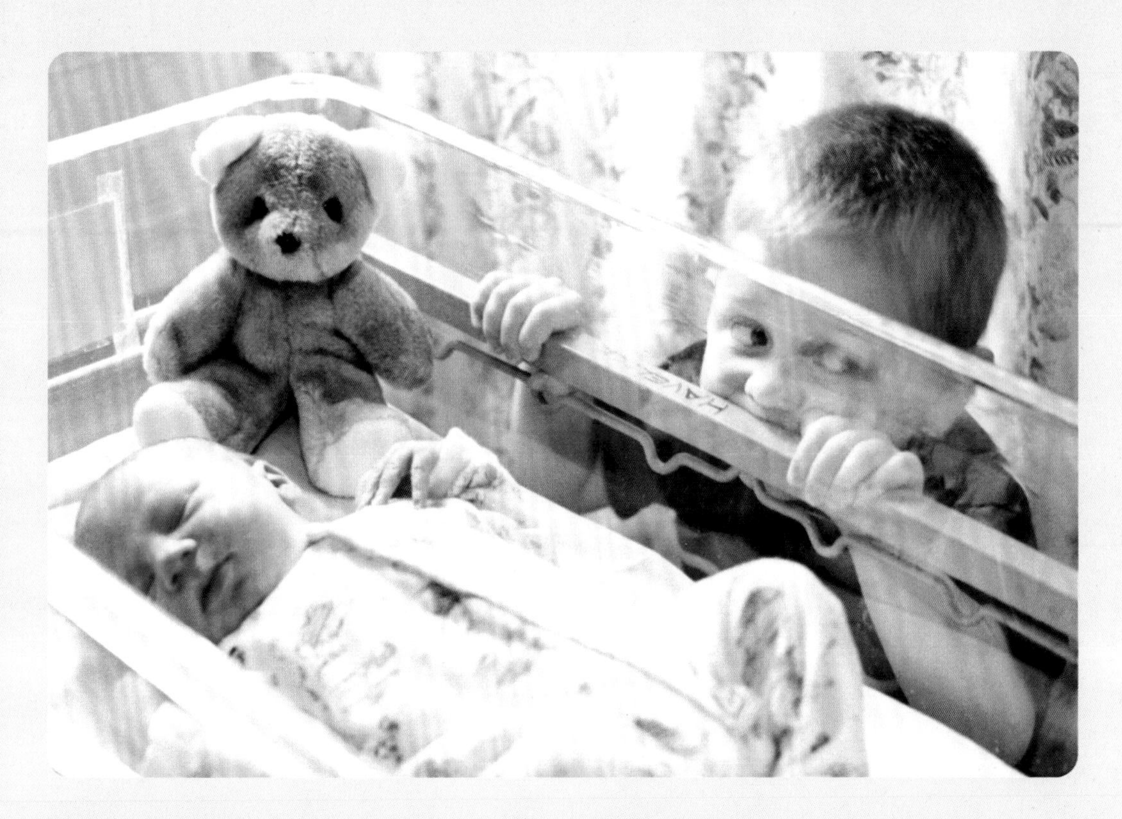

Becoming aware of others

How does your baby build up mental images of others? Initially, she will learn about her social environment almost exclusively from you, her parents, as well as other adults involved in her regular care. Through these initial relationships, she can form a template about how other people react to her and behave in general. Then, during the second half of her first year, your baby will become less exclusively focused on these immediate relationships and will start to seek the attention of others. She uses the knowledge and confidence in you that she has established over the last six months to second-guess how those around her—in particular, any older siblings—will respond to her smiles and babbles, and in most cases is rewarded with the positive attention she seeks.

Helping siblings relate to each other

Be aware there is one person in her life who may not be feeling as pleased as others are with your baby's arrival—an older sister or brother. Imagine coming home one evening to be greeted by these words from your spouse: "You don't mind, do you dear, if this adorable young lady [or man] moves in permanently with us, snuggle up in our bed when upset, and gets most of my attention for the next few months?" If you have another child, this is what the older sibling probably experienced the day your newborn took up residence in the household. Sibling rivalry is inevitable, and you have to handle it in a delicate way, making sure that your older child is given special attention and is allowed to be needy for a while, maybe even temporarily reverting to babyish behavior. These are common, normal, and healthy reactions. How you respond to the older child can affect the relationship that ultimately will develop between the two children as they grow up. For more advice on this, see pages 36–38.

The parent–child bond

For most mothers, and some fathers, feelings of love and responsibility toward their babies begin to form during pregnancy. At birth, the rush of emotions can be overwhelming, even a little daunting. Many parents have moments of doubt when they worry about whether they are up to the job of parenting or worry that something might go wrong with their babies. These are all perfectly natural reactions to the new responsibilities on hand. Luckily for adults, both the behavior and the appearance of babies seem designed to engender feelings of love and care. From the moment of birth, new emotions are awakened in parents, triggered by the cries, the smell, and the general appearance of vulnerability—features such as the big eyes—of their newborns. Thus begins the process called "bonding."

The complete dependence of a tiny baby sets the agenda for the parent–child relationship. As discussed earlier, newborns display selective attention to human faces and voices, and learn to recognize their parents in their first days. Your infant's face will brighten as she sees you approach or hears your voice. This immediately elicits love in you, and you interpret this as proof that you are special to your baby, which, in turn, strengthens the two-way relationship.

Your newborn will also display certain reflexive behaviors that, although not intentional, promote bonding. For example, she will automatically mimic some of your mouth movements, sticking her tongue out or making an "O shape" in response to seeing this being done close up. Although at this stage these responses are not intentional—the mouth movements happen in reflex, much like a yawn—to you it feels like a purposeful interaction, proof that your baby is responding to you. In return, you will respond with more smiles, vocalizations, and mouth movements, and a little "dialogue" begins, which is mutually stimulating and serves to strengthen your growing attachment.

Bonding is a two-way process

Bonding is a vital part of your new baby's development. The establishment of a secure and fulfilling relationship with her primary caregiver (usually the mother at first) paves the way for your child's future relationships, be it with other members of the family, friends, and, eventually, lifelong partners.

It is thought that the attachment between mother and baby, if close and secure, establishes in the child a basic trust of other people. Through the first attachments that a baby establishes with her parents, she is able to form an internal model of how the social world functions, which, in turn, enables her to situate herself within her environment. Such a model is based on a series of interactive experiences, accumulated from the start of life. The process is a gradual one and takes some years.

Early relationships are utterly crucial. Insecure attachments in early life can have serious long-term consequences, reflected in a failure to thrive both physically and emotionally.

Especially young babies communicate their attachment to parents through crying, smiling, eye contact, and vocalizing. In exchange, parents encourage this communication with words, cuddles, imitation of baby's facial expressions, or sounds, and through constant caregiving. Parental body language and tone of voice also play an important role. The aim of your baby's first attachment behaviors is to obtain warmth, comfort, and security. As she grows, she gradually learns how to predict your behavior.

She will manage to work out what makes you smile and what encourages you to pay even more attention to her.

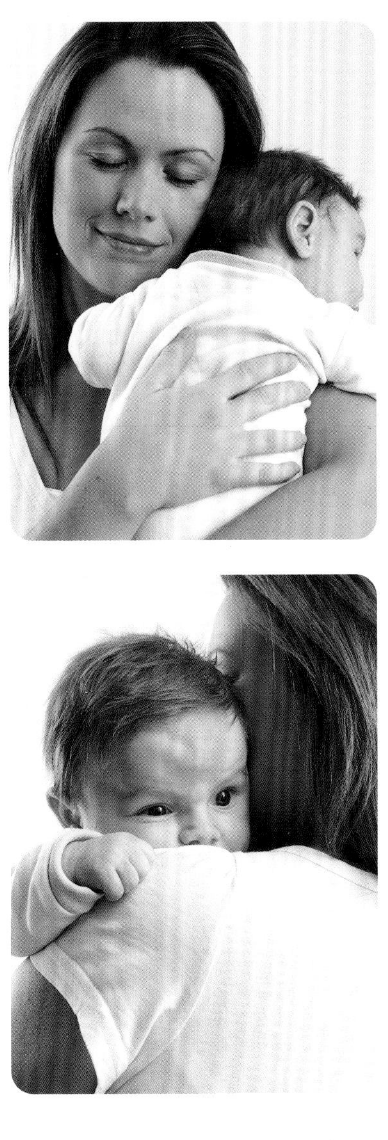

When a baby smiles

The onset of the social smile, at around two months, is a perfect example of behavior prediction. Before this age, a baby's "smile" is a muscular response to physical sensations, such as an air bubble in her stomach or the contorting of facial muscles in response to being stroked on her cheek. Your baby is not really smiling, but, for you, its resemblance to smiling is good enough to prompt you to smile in return and makes you feel loved by your baby. Once your baby learns to control her smile, she quickly begins to associate smiling with the pleasure it brings to you and others. From then onward, she will use her smile at every opportunity and will delight at the effect it has on people. Later, this repertoire will be extended as she discovers ways of making others laugh.

Strengthening the relationship

Within a few months of birth, then, your baby is already aware of the two-way flow of emotions in the parent–child relationship. She will then begin to act in ways that are specifically designed to encourage loving responses from you. For example, when you approach her crib, she may stretch out her arms, indicating her desire to be picked up and cuddled. And when you hold her, she may snuggle against your neck, embrace you with her little arms, or stroke your face.

Although you have been experiencing similar close contact with your baby since she was born, she is now a far more active participant in each interaction. This is because she is gradually gaining knowledge about the reciprocal nature of social relationships.

The strong feelings that form part of the relationship between parents and babies are not always immediately apparent. Although you may have expected to fall in love right away with your newborn and possess the maternal or paternal instincts necessary to render you instantly attuned to your baby's every need, in reality you, like many new parents, may feel quite overwhelmed by the experience of birth and the sudden presence of a newborn in your life. It can take time for feelings of love to emerge. People are not robots programmed to be instantly perfect parents, nor can love be switched on like a light. Don't worry, then, if it takes you some weeks before you really begin to feel like a mother or father. This will happen as you get to know your baby and become more attuned to your new responsibilities. Your confidence will grow naturally as you settle into your new role and learn increasingly more about how to decode your baby's behavior.

Right from the start, by simply talking to your baby and maintaining frequent physical and eye contact, you have set in place the basis for a strong bond. And you should use every opportunity to communicate with your infant.

Talking to others

While your baby will play a big role in making the parent–child bond happen automatically, if you feel that things are not as they should be, that you are unhappy or not bonding as easily as you would like, seek help, for example, from your healthcare provider or other parents. Don't bottle things up. Keep in mind that for several weeks after birth, a woman's hormone levels will still be fluctuating wildly and she will be physically exhausted. This can have a direct bearing on her emotions and ability to adjust to her new life. Many mothers experience moments of fear when they worry about the frailty of their newborns or feel clumsy and awkward handling them. These are normal reactions. If you are affected, share your feelings and worries with your partner, friends, or other new mothers—you will discover that you are not alone.

Keep in mind, too, that the father may be worrying about his ability to bond with the baby. If the mother is breastfeeding and he is out at work all day, he may feel left out. However, there are things you can do to help your baby bond with both her parents:

- Set aside some special time each day for dad and the little one to spend alone together.
- Share caregiving activities as much as possible, to be sure that your baby learns how both her parents feel, smell, and sound and gets to know that daddy is also there to provide her with what she needs. This should include every aspect of care: feeding, bathing, changing, and putting to bed.
- Also, why not set the alarm a little earlier than necessary each morning so that the three of you, as a family, can snuggle up in bed before the start of the working day?

LOOKING AHEAD

PROXIMITY-SEEKING

As your baby becomes mobile, the world will take on a whole new meaning. With the ability to move away from you, comes new anxieties and a need for security. You will find that whenever she is in a new situation, she will regularly check where you are and seek proximity to you. Proximity-seeking is a sign of a healthy, secure parent–child bond, and it should not be interpreted as shyness. In fact, it is the most securely attached babies who show the greatest confidence in exploring new things. When your baby finds herself in an unfamiliar room, she will confine herself to an area a safe distance away from you. You then become a "secure base" from which she can happily explore. Every few minutes she will turn and seek eye or physical contact, or just check that you are still there to reassure herself that it is safe to continue her activities.

Acquiring a sense of self

Understanding that one is a separate being with individual thoughts, feelings, needs, and desires is a complicated process. It starts when a baby gets to know her own body and progresses with her learning to recognize her own reflection. The process involves acknowledging other people as separate beings with minds and bodies of their own, as well as understanding the different terms used to refer to oneself and others: "me," "I," "you," and "they." Not surprisingly, then, self-awareness is a lengthy, complicated journey that begins in infancy and spans the whole of toddlerhood.

Little is known about an infant's knowledge of her own body. While still in the womb, your baby discovered the feel and taste of her thumb, may have touched her feet, or even joined hands. However, it's not possible to say that at this stage she had formed any kind of mental representation of what she looked like. Such prenatal activity is reflex driven, occurring largely by chance. At birth, your baby's movements are still mainly reflex driven, but within a few weeks, she will gain enough control to start playing with her hands and feet and discovering how they look, taste, and move. These body parts act as convenient, constantly available playthings, entertaining her even when you are not around. At this stage, however, the learning process involves little more than your baby finding out about the many interesting parts she has and can move—discoveries that let her brain form a sensory map of her body. A true sense of what her body looks like, and a basic understanding of what it can do as a whole system, will not emerge until your child begins to develop a self-concept (see page 30).

Learning through play

Your baby discovers how her body works, looks, and feels through exploration and play. She should never be discouraged from doing so, even if it causes embarrassment to you. Finding out about her own body is an important part of your baby's development, becuase it helps her to distinguish herself from others. Her sense of individuality, gender, independence, and self-control emerges via the process of coming to know herself, as well as her interaction with others. Your baby needs the freedom to find out about every aspect of her body—what each part does, and how it feels, smells, and tastes—and should be encouraged to do so.

Bath time offers the perfect opportunity for looking at arms and legs, hands and feet, belly button, and anything else on her body or yours that might be interesting. Try to give your little one some regular time undressed or just wearing a diaper for free play (maybe lying on a towel) before you rush to put fresh clothes on her. Through this kind of play, she can gradually build a mental image of who and what she is. This exploration will encourage her to build a confident and unashamed attitude toward her body and nakedness and the individual characteristics that make her unique.

When infants are born, they don't make a clear distinction between themselves and the

CHILD'S VIEW OF THE HUMAN FORM

Scientists have tried to understand how young children perceive the human body by looking at their early drawings. At around two and a half, toddlers begin to draw people. These early scribbles usually consist of only a head and legs. Researchers call this the "tadpole" representation of the human body. There are several different theories regarding why toddlers represent people in this way. Some have suggested that it reflects an incomplete knowledge of the human body. However, if asked to name the different parts of the body, toddlers easily identify the arms, belly, hands, fingers, and toes, as well as the depicted head and legs. They can also successfully put together a simple puzzle of a person's head, torso, arms, and legs. So why do they draw people with only heads and legs?

Drawing is a complicated task for the especially young child. To produce a drawing, a toddler's arms, hands, and fingers have to be controlled and carefully coordinated, and the toddler must make the connection between moving a pencil with her hand and producing a line on the paper. To then translate what she is seeing into a series of associated movements that will create a comparable drawing is extremely difficult. Therefore, it is thought that when drawing a human, the young artist selects features that are both important and, when put together, produce a balanced and well-proportioned representation in the simplest and most manageable way possible. You have already read how important faces are to babies. Adding long legs to the head is the easiest way to give the head a "body" and provide the drawing with spatial realism.

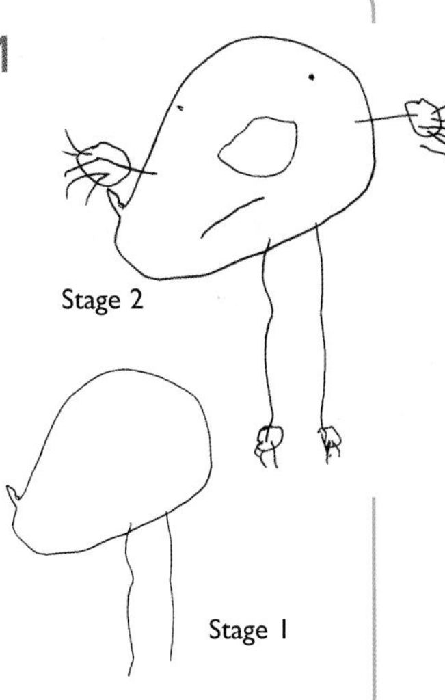

Another theory that has been put forward suggests that the tadpole drawing is an abstract depiction of the human body. Early drawings of people are produced at a time when young children are engaging in active symbolic play, where a nest of pillows can represent a ship, or the underneath of a table can be a mysterious cave. One could, therefore, expect the same type of abstraction and imagination in drawing. However, without being able to actually see through a baby's eyes, it is impossible for us to really know how babies perceive themselves and others.

rest of their environment. In other words, they are not entirely sure where their bodies end and the rest of the world—the objects and people around them—begins. Finding out how their own bodies feel, look, and move is the first step to acquiring self-awareness.

The emergence of "me"

A baby's concept of self develops gradually. It is a product of the interaction between her and her physical and social environments. It begins with her ability to place herself, or more specifically, her body, within the immediate environment. At birth, your infant's actions are largely reflex driven and involuntary. Day by day, however, her brain learns to form links between her automatic actions (turns head toward the sound of a barking dog) and their outcomes (sees dog wagging his tail). In time, these links will prompt voluntary actions and increasing control over behavior, so that placed again in the same situation, your baby will now turn to look for the dog before it has even barked. Once she has gained some control over her body and its actions, your baby is able to start placing herself mentally within her surroundings, making the distinction between herself and others. She learns that although she is completely dependent on those around her for her care and well-being, she is nevertheless an autonomous being who can act alone and influence those around her.

The foundations of this knowledge, this understanding of "me" as a concept, start to emerge at around six months. It takes a long time to fully develop, and it is only at around two years of age that your child's self-concept will be clearly expressed through her use of words, such as "I," "me," or "mine," that allow her to communicate directly her sense of self. Prior to these language clues, how can you discern self-awareness in a baby? One way you can assess this is to examine her responses to her mirror image.

Self-awareness *can be demonstrated by whether your baby is able to identify that there is a red spot where it shouldn't be.*

Looking at reflections in a mirror

During the first three months of life, an infant shows little interest in her own reflection—it is just something to look at, much like the other faces on the television screen. Unlike her mommy's or daddy's interesting faces, it doesn't even say anything; it just stares back. This is why young babies quickly lose interest in their own reflections when you hold them up to a mirror.

By about four months, however, there is a noticeable change. Your baby will gradually become more interested in what she sees in mirrors and may even reach out toward an object appearing in a reflection. At this stage, however, she has yet to understand the link between the reflection and the real thing. She will still stare at her own face in the mirror in much the same way as she will stare at yours. There seems to be no indication that your baby knows that she is looking at her own face. This can be tested by watching her reaction to her mirror reflection as you make a visible object, such as a toy, approach from behind: at four months of age, your baby will not turn around to look for the object but will expect it to be in front of her.

Between four and eight months, however, your baby will become increasingly interested in what she sees in mirrors and will often smile at her own reflection. Don't worry—this is not an early indication of vanity. At this stage, she is probably still unsure who she is smiling at, because it is only after she is ten months old that her spatial awareness is developed enough to let her grasp the nature of mirror reflections.

When your baby is 11 months old, hold her in front of a mirror and try the toy experiment again; she will now turn to see what's approaching from behind. Your child can now understand that what she is seeing is a reflection. However, turning to look for the toy doesn't necessarily mean that she knows the face in the mirror is hers; she simply understands that what she is looking at is not the real thing. This step indicates a development in her spatial representation of the immediate environment. She has formed a mental picture of her environment and recognizes that it is the same as the one in the mirror. So she uses this information to situate the approaching toy in relation to the rest of the things around her.

Evidence suggests that at this stage a baby has yet to form in her mind a clear picture or memory of her own face. We know this because if a red spot is surreptitiously painted onto a ten-month-old baby's forehead before she looks in the mirror, she will not attempt to rub it off when she sees her own reflection. It takes another six to eight months before she will make the connection between what she is seeing (a red spot on the forehead of her reflection), and what is on her face at that moment. By eighteen months of age, however, she will immediately bring her hand up to her forehead to touch the red spot. This is a clear demonstration of self-awareness.

Although scientists still have to pinpoint the exact mechanisms involved in gaining a self-image, research with primates shows that day-to-day interaction with others plays an important role in self-awareness. Chimpanzees are one of the only other species to display self-recognition of their mirror reflections. Interestingly, however, young chimps brought up in complete social isolation, away from other chimpanzees and devoid of social interaction, never develop self-recognition. It seems that without the constant feedback we get from others around us, developing a self-concept is particularly difficult.

So although the actual process by which your child will come to develop a self-image remains to some extent a mystery, we know that it is through getting to know her body and studying other people in relation to herself that she is ultimately able to work out who and what she is.

PLAYING MIRROR GAMES

From 4 to 6 months

Hold your baby within arm's reach of a mirror and have your partner or a friend approach with a toy from behind, so that your baby can clearly see the toy in the mirror reflection but not out of the corner of her eye. It is also important that she doesn't hear the person doing it. Encourage her to respond to what she is looking at with prompts such as: "Where's the toy?" or "Can you see the toy?" A common response will be for your baby to reach out to the mirror reflection of the approaching toy, paying little attention to her own face in the mirror. After you get that response, try making a noise with the toy. Your baby will turn to look at it. Then hide the toy, attract the baby's attention back to the mirror, and again let the toy approach silently. This hide-and-seek exercise can be fun for everyone. You can actively take part in and follow your little one's learning process. As her self-awareness grows and she works out the cause-and-effect rules of the game, she will learn to anticipate your next move and eventually catch you.

From 6 months

Your baby will grow increasingly communicative with the mirror images she sees. She will love to smile and gurgle at reflections of faces. Play peekaboo in the mirror, talk to your baby as she watches your reflection, or just let her study her own face quietly.

From 10 months

Try the approaching toy test again (see 4 to 6 months). It is easier to do alone, now that she can sit up unaided. By this age, you can expect her to turn around and look for the toy, even if you have never done the test before.

From 1 year

Try the red spot experiment. Apply a red spot gently on baby's forehead or on the end of her nose while she's sleeping or distracted enough with something else that she will not notice you've done it. Use something easily removable and not harmful to your baby's delicate skin, such as eye shadow. Don't use a sticker because it poses a choking hazard, and your baby may feel its sticky presence on her forehead

before she looks in the mirror. Make sure you leave some time between putting the red spot on and showing her the mirror, so that she makes no direct connection between the two acts. Once she sees her reflection, does she point at the spot in the mirror? Or does she attempt to rub it off immediately? What do you think her reaction indicates? Is she recognizing herself instantly or does it take time for her to realize her face doesn't look like it usually does?

Another variation of this little game shows your baby's memory for your face. Try placing a funny sticker on your face while your baby is looking in the mirror—without her seeing you do this, of course. Then see if she turns around to examine your face when she sees your reflection with its new addition.

Discovering gender

At what point in development does a child realize she is a girl or he is a boy? To us, gender seems self-evident, an indisputable and obvious characteristic we're born with and are aware of from the start, but it is different with children.

It isn't until toddlers reach about three years of age that they develop a comprehensive gender concept and really understand that there are two categories of people—male and female—and they belong to only one.

Having said that, babies start learning about certain important sex-typing characteristics from the day they are born.

Scientists have been able to show that long before they reach their first birthdays, babies can already discriminate between stereotyped photos of male and female faces. They have formed a basic gender category based on particular cues, such as hairlines, facial features, and facial hair. Interestingly, even at one month, infants can correctly match a female voice with a female face, as long as both the voice and face are highly stereotyped (such as high-pitched voice matched with smooth face, slender jawline, and long hair). However, it is not until several months later that they can correctly match the sound of a male voice to a male-looking face. This is probably due to the fact that mothers tend to be the primary caregivers during the first few months of life, which gives

babies the chance to learn more about female characteristics than male. However, if a dad happens to be the main carer, his baby would probably discriminate male feature types first.

To match a voice to a face, your baby needs to be able to make difficult connections between what she hears and sees. It is only after repeated exposure to male and female voices and facial features, and sufficient opportunities to compare them, that your baby can piece together some knowledge about their differences.

Gender-related behavior

Although babies are actively learning about gender during their first eighteen months, it is difficult to ascertain precisely how much they know until the latter half of their second year, when they exhibit pronounced sex-typed behavior in general interaction and during play. Your toddler will probably start to use the labels "girl" and "boy" correctly with respect both to herself and to others (adults, siblings, and peers) some time in her third year. However, it isn't until her third birthday that she will be able to communicate her understanding of gender permanence and consistency. This can be tested by asking your daughter questions, such as: "Have you ever been a boy?" and "Were you a boy when you were born?" or "When you are grown up, will you be a mommy or a daddy?" Three is also the age at which you may begin to notice stronger gender stereotyping in your child's general behavior, play activities, choice of toys, and even choice of friends.

Although there are obviously exceptions, many three-year-old girls will select sedentary and constructive play, such as tea parties, constructions, and puzzles, and will be more inclined to ask what role or game another child would like to play. In contrast, many little boys will engage in more physical rough-and-tumble play, refuse to take on certain roles, such as the nurse in a doctors-and-nurses game, and choose trucks instead of dolls to play with.

The important point to make is that despite attempts by parents to bring up their young children in a nonstereotypical environment—buying cars for girls or dolls for boys, or encouraging boys to take part in quiet creative play at the expense of loud or active fun, while thrusting footballs at little girls—by a young age, children have already learned to categorize what seems appropriate and inappropriate to their gender role. What's more, the majority of these learned distinctions are unwittingly and subtly provided by you, the parent.

How parents influence gender typing

Even a young baby will begin to note the differences between the way her parents behave in everyday life, the way they react to the child, and to her particular behavior. You are, therefore, your child's primary source of gender-type information. A basic finding, for instance, is that adults tend to hold female infants more gently than males of the same age.

Unbeknown to the child (and often to the adults in question), parents have usually formed a gender-specific idea of their child even before his or her birth.

Parents-to-be often speculate about the sex of their unborn baby: "He kicks so vigorously, he must be a footballer."

Think about the first question one asks of a newborn: "Is it a boy or girl?" From that moment onward, the baby's sex will determine to a significant degree how people behave toward her and what her future holds.

We all like to think that we are beyond stereotypes, but a wealth of research shows that parental beliefs and behavior are clearly affected by certain intrinsic gender-related attitudes. In one experiment, expectant parents were told the sex of several youngsters of nine months to three years and asked to rate the infants using gender-type characteristics. The babies pictured were labeled "boy" or "girl," and the adults were asked to rate how "strong" or "weak," "active" or "inactive" each infant was. Results showed that the adults' ratings coincided far more with the label given (boy or girl) than the child's actual characteristics.

Other data has shown that parents are more likely to describe newborn girls as "smaller," "softer," and more "fragile" and as having "finer features" than newborn boys, irrespective of whether this is really true. In fact, apart from the genitals, there are no obvious physical differences between male and female newborns. Additional research has demonstrated that if you show a group of adults a video recording of a baby dressed in blue, moving around in a crib, they will interpret the baby's movements as being typical of a burly boy. However, if the same baby's clothes are changed to pink by straightforward video editing, the adults will interpret exactly the same behavior as typical of dainty girls.

Studies comparing the ways mothers and fathers interact and play with boy and girl toddlers have shown that, however unintentionally, parents often encourage certain gender-type activities. In the groups filmed as part of the research, fathers were more probable to initiate rougher play with boys but to engage in quiet, nonintrusive play with girls, while mothers were found to regularly reward appropriate gender-related behavior. For example, they would show marked enthusiasm when a baby girl chose nurturing games, such as fantasy play with dolls, or when a baby boy engaged in construction-type play with blocks. Both parents would also unwittingly steer each child toward playing with certain toys as opposed to others, according to his or her sex.

In general, findings from this type of research demonstrate that parental behavior, attitudes, and expectations become progressively more gender specific the older a child gets.

The sibling bond

The road to becoming a social being starts within the family, where the first bonds are created. These provide the foundations for all future relationships. One of the most difficult to forge is the sibling bond, which is filled with jealousy and competition from the start. It is up to you, as a parent, to carefully manage and promote the positive development of this particularly special, lifelong relationship.

Preparing older children for a sibling

It's always important to involve the older child, or children, as early as possible—ideally, your pregnancy is established and really showing—don't wait until the day you bring the new baby home. Even if an older child is not yet speaking, show him your baby bump and talk to him about it. Point out babies when you pass them in the street and explain that mommy is carrying one inside her. Involve your child in the preparations at home before the birth; for example, let him investigate the nursery equipment.

If you need to implement changes that particularly affect your older child, such as moving him into a proper bed to free the crib for the baby, do so sensitively and in plenty of time. If possible, put these changes into effect several months before the birth. Make a big fuss of him; perhaps let him be involved in choosing the new bed or bedding, or in helping to reorganize the room. Leave a gap of several weeks, if possible, before "giving" your new baby the vacated crib. This way, your eldest will not feel ousted, and the transition to the new bed will remain a positive instead of negative move.

Nearer the end of your pregnancy, decide where your child will be while you are giving birth. Some older children show great interest in attending a birth, and this is a family decision. However, young toddlers will probably be better off with grandparents or friends, away from the upsetting sight of mommy in pain.

When the baby arrives

Initially, your new baby will have eyes only for her main caregivers. Your infant will barely notice an older sibling and this can be a disappointment to your eldest, who has been preparing himself for the baby's arrival for months. After only a few weeks, however, your youngest will learn to recognize her sibling's face and voice, along with others she sees and hears on a regular basis. Although she will not yet actively seek her sibling's attention at this age, it isn't too soon for your eldest to seek hers.

It can take weeks or even months for the effect on the older sibling to become evident. Most parents find that there is an initial "honeymoon period" when the older sibling seems unaffected. This is because, at first, the toddler may either be fascinated by, or completely disinterested in, the newborn. Both reactions are normal. At this point, the older child is still unsure whether or not this new person is a permanent thing in his life. Mom and Dad are making an effort to keep things as normal as possible around the home, he's getting special attention, the baby is asleep most of the time, she doesn't touch his toys—this is not so bad.

Helping your first born

The best way for you to help your firstborn cope with the new arrival is to try to put yourself in his shoes as often as possible. The role of sibling is a heavy responsibility for a child to shoulder. So remind yourself often that the transition for your firstborn from singleton to sibling is a difficult one that takes a lot of adjusting to. A child as young as one year of age may be acutely aware of the sudden alterations that have taken place not just in day-to-day life but also in the place he now holds within the family unit.

Responding to behavior changes

Within a few weeks of a new baby's arrival, when the novelty wears off and the realization dawns on your older child that the new intruder is here to stay, you may experience a backlash. This can happen suddenly or it can take the form of more gradual changes in your child's behavior. Many new siblings revert to babyish habits that you probably were hoping had disappeared for good (thumb-sucking, waking at night, wetting the bed, or wanting to return to diapers or a bottle, refusing to eat, etc.). Don't worry. These are only temporary relapses. The important thing is for you to remain calm and to try not to react, if possible.

Instead of reacting to a tantrum, go back over the event that triggered it and try to see how the situation might have felt for your eldest. Remember that, right now, his position in the family probably feels somewhat precarious. He is looking for ways to reestablish his place in the home and reclaim your now-divided attention. And he will use every means available. This can be frustrating for parents, especially when you are also trying to cope with the constant demands of a new baby.

The arrival of a sibling is one of the most significant and life-changing events of childhood. Your older child's self-confidence will be undermined by the changes that take place, and becoming dependent again is the only way he can be assured of competing for your time. Your aim should be to communicate that infantile behavior is not the way for him to get your attention. Instead, you should try the following:

- Make a special point of reinforcing any positive behavior, however trivial.
- Congratulate your child for doing the opposite to the undesired behavior.
- Reward him for showing any kind of positive interest or patience toward the baby.
- Put regular time aside each day that you can devote to your eldest on his own.

This phase, during which your older child is rebuilding his identity and place within the family, requires you to do what may seem obvious but is often hard to achieve when two or more little children are screaming at once; remain the adult, stay calm and in control, and when it gets too much, seek help.

Making time for the older child

If you are experiencing difficulties in getting your toddler used to his new brother or sister, there are several things you can try. You and everyone around (relatives, caregivers,

teachers, and family friends) need to be especially encouraging and supportive of the older sibling. His self-esteem will be shaken by the arrival of a baby, and he needs to feel confident that he is still loved by those around him. Make a point of being particularly interested in his activities. Both parents should apportion special time each day to spend alone with him, away from the baby.

It is important that after the birth, your child's routines should carry on as normally as possible. Cutting out the bedtime story because baby is hungry at that time of day may not seem important to you, but to your older child it would be upsetting. Organize treats or trips out to make him feel special and plan in advance so that you can optimize your time with him. Whenever possible, involve him in activities surrounding the baby or around the house in general. If he feels he is helping mom or dad in ways that the baby cannot, his self-confidence will then be boosted.

Helping children to engage with each other

Although initially the baby appeared to take little notice of her older sibling, by two months of age she will be increasingly responsive to her visual environment. Her interest in toys and other colorful or noisy objects means that, if your older child now shows his little sister his prize possessions, he probably will get a noticeable response. Such sibling interaction should be encouraged from the start. You'll be surprised at how much pleasure your older child can get from a simple gurgle or smile from the baby. Even getting the baby to actively follow his moving toy is a satisfying game for a sibling to play.

Peekaboo and other little games that involve an element of surprise are more probable to prompt excited reactions, so teach your older child how to safely entertain his sister as soon as he shows interest in doing so. The more mutually satisfying exchanges they experience, the more probable it will be that they form a close bond.

During childhood, siblings often end up spending as much time, if not more, with each other as they do with their parents, so the interaction between children has a significant impact on their later development.

This bond plays a role in the acquisition of language, play, the development of attachment, as well as a child's general understanding of how the world works. Infants' responses to their brothers or sisters have been little studied; unfortunately, research into sibling relationships has tended to concentrate on older children's reactions to the arrival of a new baby and on sibling rivalry. However, what has been clearly shown is that older siblings can have a positive impact on babies. They not only provide constant stimulation but also act as role models, paving the way for learning and socializing. By the second half of your baby's first year, she will be actively seeking her brother's attention, and this is when you can really encourage interaction between the two.

Becoming aware of strangers

As your baby's social world expands beyond her immediate home environment, she will naturally experience some anxieties. The first noticeable phase will emerge in the second half of her first year and is generally referred to as "fear of strangers." This involves a new and sudden reluctance by your baby to interact with, to be held by, or even to approach people with whom she isn't 100 percent familiar. This new wariness can come as a surprise to parents. An up-to-now confident baby, who enjoyed nothing more than smiling and babbling at everyone, seems to become transformed overnight into a fearful, shy, tearful child.

Especially young infants will readily snuggle up in any willing arms and let one and all attend to them. At that early stage, a baby is not yet aware of the complexities of her environment. Her day-to-day life revolves around her basic needs. It is only as her cognitive skills develop, as she begins to perceive her physical and social world as a complicated and constantly changing place, and as her bonds with her parents grow deeper, that she develops certain fears.

Showing inhibition in public and refusing to approach unfamiliar people is a healthy coping mechanism.

It is both an expression of emerging anxieties and a means of protection, because it prompts mommy or daddy to come to the rescue.

The onset of stranger-awareness coincides with various new developments, including the ability to form clear memories of an increasing number of individual faces, voices, and behaviors. This is an important stage to have reached. Your baby now has stored in her mind detailed images of the people with whom she regularly spends time. These can be used as internal templates against which other people are matched. When someone she doesn't know well approaches now, she is able to quickly realize that this is not someone for whom she possesses memories, and this naturally causes her to feel uncertain and apprehensive. Fear of strangers, therefore, is not an indication of a shy temperament. It is simply an expression of your baby's growing awareness and knowledge of her immediate world. As this knowledge strengthens and expands, she will realize that new people and situations aren't so different. She will learn to interpret and anticipate the behavior of others and understand that in the vast majority of cases they are not to be feared.

Helping an anxious baby

Stranger-anxiety is a fairly short-lived phase, lasting a few months at most. During this time, it is important not to force new people and situations onto your baby. She needs to find balance within herself and to discover at her own pace how to deal with her anxieties. Gentle encouragement, comfort, and plenty of patience are the best remedies. As your baby's social experiences continue to diversify, these anxieties are progressively overcome but may, at times, be replaced by new ones. When she's older and more confident about the tangible things that make up her world, she may gradually develop anxieties about imaginary threats, such as monsters or ghosts. However, she may go through recurring stages of fear of strangers as she progresses through her social world. For example, renewed fears may surface when your child starts nursery and she faces her peers alone for the first time.

So don't be surprised if your little one swings between gregarious confidence and shyness as she becomes more independent and finds her place in the social world.

Separation anxiety

It may seem paradoxical, but the closer and more securely attached children are to their parents, the easier it is for them to become independent.

A child who feels safe, and who knows that she can always rely on her carers to be there and offer comfort and guidance whenever she needs them is far more likely to have the confidence to actively explore the world. Hugs and reassurance don't make for a nervous, dependent baby. On the contrary, they encourage youngsters to be more explorative and help them learn to build trust in others, an important precursor to forming friendships. All this starts early in the first year of life, when infants discover that they are part of a family, be it with one-parent, two-parents, or extended. The number isn't important. What counts is that infants feel loved and cared for by adults who are consistent in their responses and sensitive to their needs. It is these early interactions that form the foundation for later relationships in life.

A child's coping mechanism

From about one year onward, your young child may start to display anxious behavior—crying, screaming, shouting, kicking—when she sees or even anticipates you leaving. This is a normal response to separation. What your child is reacting to is the fact that her secure attachment with you is temporarily under threat. By protesting, she is making sure that you will return to comfort her and maybe reduces the likelihood that you will leave again. In some ways, then, your child is actively trying to restore the equilibrium by "punishing" you for leaving her alone. At this age, she doesn't yet possess the words to communicate her feelings, so the only coping strategy available to her is to cry or make a fuss. Typically, she will become agitated and then upset upon seeing you leave the room. She may not consent to being consoled by another adult, but will remain distraught or distracted until you return. When you do return, your child will show great enthusiasm or may resort to clinginess. In some cases, she may continue crying for a little while in order to be held, but once she is satisfied that you are here to stay, she will return to playing happily.

This is the time when more than ever you are used as a "secure base" (see the box, page 27). You will notice your little one turning often, as she plays or explores her surroundings, to check your whereabouts and make sure that

Mixing with others *from an early age, whether at a nursery or play group or with a childminder, may help to prevent separation anxiety.*

she has your attention. Separation anxiety occurs in most young children who have developed a secure bond or attachment to their parents. In fact, psychologists have found that a child's display of separation anxiety can be used as a reliable measure of the strength of her attachments—a predictive tool for later development, because early attachments are the prototype of later relationships.

Other influences, however, can also play a role in how your child will react in new situations, so it is important to keep these in mind, too. For example, her temperament will have an impact on how she responds to a novel environment—some children are naturally more adventurous, whereas others are more cautious. The way you respond to such differences will also affect her behavior; for example, if you pay too much attention to your child's "complaints," this will reinforce her negative reaction to being left. Furthermore, early experiences can have a direct bearing on how your baby interprets being left alone, even for a brief moment. For instance, if your baby is regularly cared for by several different people from a young age (grandparents, siblings, babysitters, friends), she may not display as strong a reaction to separation as a baby who is looked after primarily by one parent.

To sum up, context, mood, physical well-being on the day, and her background will all have a bearing on how your baby reacts to new experiences, as well as to separation from and reunion with you.

The theory of mind

As your child gets older, relationships outside the family will increasingly gain importance. Relationships within the home environment are relatively dependent in nature; when your little one is with someone she knows, she can, to some extent, predict his or her behavior and is comfortable with the fact that the person she is interacting with—be it parent, carer, or sibling—is the dominant partner in the exchange. In the wider world, however, with peers and others with whom she will have more transient relations, she will have to second-guess their responses and manage her own behavior accordingly. She will begin to understand that other people have minds, too—ideas, intentions, and feelings of their own—that affect the way they behave, think, and act. This understanding, generally referred to as "theory of mind," is one of the most important characteristics that sets humans apart from other species.

Observing others and learning to predict their behavior will be one of the most difficult hurdles your child has to overcome, because the boundaries of her social world continue to expand. This is why playing with other children and making friends will be far from straightforward. As a parent, you can encourage this learning process by making sure that, from the time she is mobile, your baby will have regular opportunities to meet and spend time with other children and grown-ups. You will also need to stay sensitive to her anxieties at all times. Forcing sociability on a child who is afraid of strangers or experiencing separation anxiety will only exacerbate her problems.

Theory of mind involves attributing thoughts to others and viewing their actions as a function of these thoughts. If you suddenly see someone opening and closing one drawer after another, you don't think that he or she is simply doing that for no reason; you think that such actions indicate that the individual has lost something. In other words, theory of mind entails interpreting people's behavior in terms of their intentions and what they think instead of just what they do.

How it develops

Research into the development of theory of mind in children shows that it progresses through two stages. The first covers roughly the first six months of life, and involves babies realizing that people are "intentional agents" who behave according to intentions or goals. Even the simplest of activities, such as following another person's gaze or playing peekaboo, involves trying to predict an outcome and anticipate what a person will do next.

One of the first ways your infant experiences intentionality is by following your gaze—an activity that takes up much of her waking time. By gauging the direction you are looking in, locating what you are looking at and watching your actions, she comes to realize that when you turn your head to look at a toy, you will probably then go and pick up the toy.

The next thing your baby discovers is that she can actually use her gaze to direct other people's attention. If she wants something that is out of reach, for instance, by catching your attention, and then looking intently at the desired object and back at you several times, she can communicate her desire for you to get it for her well before she can speak. This is referred to as establishing "joint attention." It is something we adults do naturally but, for a baby, it involves making smart links between people's behaviors and their outcomes.

By the age of one year, your baby will be good at this, although she will not yet have realized that mental intentions do not always match the situations or people's behavior.

Theory of mind *can, among other things, enable your child to engage in more constructive play with another, because he'll be able to understand what his friend is attempting to do.*

She has yet to understand that people can hold wrong beliefs, tell lies, or deceive one another.

Behavior related to thought

This is the second stage in the process of developing a theory of mind. Being somewhat more complex than the previous stage, it takes another two to three years to become fully established and involves your young child seeing people in a new light. No longer does she see people simply as intentional agents whose behavior is a function of the goals they have, but as mental agents with thoughts and beliefs that may lead them to behave in unpredictable ways. In other words, she has progressed from being able to understand that others have goals to having to predict what they will do on the basis of what they think.

Imagine the following: You've put the keys on the chair and your partner moves them to the table when you are out of the room. When you come back, where will you look for your keys? On the table where they actually are, or on the chair where you *think* they are? Understanding that you will look where you think they are is what understanding other minds is all about. Once your child realizes that people behave according to their thoughts, she can start lying, because she then appreciates that she can influence your thinking by what she says and that you will act on those thoughts. Before that, when your child seems to be lying ("I didn't do it"), she is really trying to avoid consequences, not sow untruths into your mind.

So, being able to lie, to deceive, or sabotage another's goals, however irritating that can be, is actually a huge step forward developmentally. It is what makes us truly social beings and allows us to feel empathy and compassion for what others may be feeling or thinking.

Teasing and humor

Children laugh long before they can speak, and the progression of humor—from peekaboo games to clapping hands or hiding and grabbing away; to playing tricks and deceiving; and, finally, using word riddles and jokes—coincides loosely with the different stages of physical and intellectual development.

Humor helps babies to learn to interact with others and manage emotions; it assists in problem solving and is a vital part of growing up in the social world.

From the age of about three months, babies begin to recognize the difference between angry versus pleased tones of voice and facial expressions. At this stage, however, they do not understand the true meanings behind them; they just know that one expression differs from the other. Once a baby is able to intentionally smile and laugh, she has the means not only to communicate her enjoyment and pleasure, but to cause others to smile and laugh, too. This is an important step in social development; your baby is now involved in much more reciprocal interaction, in which she can express her burgeoning character and actively engage others in a mutually pleasing exchange.

Teaching your baby about humor

Parents naturally interact with their infants in ways that encourage humor. When you cause your baby to be alert, to smile, or chuckle, it is visible proof that you are stimulating your baby in a positive way. So all this time, just by

Hiding games, *such as those of holding and grabbing away, are teasing games that enable your baby to predict your own and others' responses.*

playing hiding games, such as peekaboo, by tickling her, or making faces and funny sounds, you have been encouraging your baby to learn about humor.

Toward the end of her first year, your baby's memory will have developed enough for her to be able to remember a whole repertoire of behaviors that will result in the kind of attention she likes best: extra hugs, praise, smiles, and laughter. She may attempt to mimic the little games you play with her—introducing her own versions of peekaboo by hiding herself under blankets or hoods or teasing you by holding out a toy and then grabbing it away just as you're about to take it. Teasing games not only form part of learning how to predict other people's responses but also test the notions of giving and sharing.

Although these games can begin as early as six months, it will be some time before your baby will actually happily give you her toy so you can play with it yourself; teasing you does not entail having to actually give up her possessions. In fact, the toy is largely incidental in this act. Neither is she trying to fool you by making you believe you will get the toy and then withdrawing it from your reach. At this early stage, teasing games are simply imitations of behavior that your baby knows will result in laughter. Real deception comes much later.

Learning by imitation

Much of early humor is based on imitation. Your baby watches and learns the behaviors that cause people (herself included) to smile and laugh, and re-creates them to produce the same effects. From teasing, once your little one is more mobile and daring, she will progress to "slapstick"-type humor, acting silly or doing absurd things to cause laughter, such as putting a plate on her head and pretending that it's a hat, dancing in a crazy way, or using funny voices.

Your baby's humor is affected by the way she plays, and during her second and third years, pretend play really takes off. She now

has the means to make the most of her imagination to prompt smiles and laughter. However, verbal humor will take a lot longer to appear. Manipulating language to make jokes is something that occurs only after your child has a confident grasp of the words she uses to communicate her needs and desires.

One of the earliest "jokes" you will probably be treated to is the purposeful misuse of names or labels—calling a dog a cat in jest, or referring to mommy as daddy—simple reversals that your baby knows will be understood as humor. Making up nonsense words at around two and a half or three is another favorite language-game toddlers like to play—a fail-safe way to bring giggles to a conversation.

Deceptive behavior

Imagine playing poker without realizing that your opponent had a hidden agenda and that you, in turn, needed to hide your intentions. Almost certainly you would not win many hands. During your day-to-day life, you constantly calculate, predict, and try to influence the behavior of others—when you play games, engage in business, or simply interact. Most of the time, you do it without even giving it a second thought. You use tactics and knowledge about other people's thoughts and beliefs to make this possible. Children begin to learn about these hidden dimensions of social life at a surprisingly early age.

Even before your toddler has fully mastered language, she can display some signs of deceptive-like behavior. Much of it develops out of what she will learn through play and from humor, and from other situations that require her to predict and manipulate other people's thoughts and expectations. For example, she may pretend to be hurt or frightened so that she will get an extra hug. You shouldn't see this form of manipulation as "lying" per se. At this age, your child is not concerned with what you actually think or believe, nor trying to sow false beliefs into your mind. She is merely acting out a habitual scene that she knows will elicit the predicted, desired response. If, however, she were to hide your keys under the pillow when you turned your back and then pretend she had not seen them when you asked about them, you could conclude that she was intentionally trying to make you hold a false belief. However, this level of understanding about other people's beliefs isn't usually reached until your child is around three or four years of age.

Lies and untruths

Children progress through several stages of "lying" before being able really to deceive others successfully. Early examples are often amusing. For instance, a toddler may state assertively: "I didn't spill the juice, and I won't do it again." This early form of cover-up is designed to avoid punishment, not to sow false thoughts in your mind.

Young children also tell untruths to boost their self-image. For example, your child may brag to her little friends about fictitious toys she owns or abilities she has. However, while these crude forms of deception may seem harmless and even entertaining to you, they should be discouraged. Be careful not to reinforce this behavior by responding to it with extra attention or amusement. Having said that, the development and use of deceptive behavior can actually be seen as a positive sign intellectually, in that it shows that your child is gaining an increasingly sophisticated understanding of other people's minds.

Making friends

During your baby's second year of life, she will become increasingly mobile and adventurous. The experiences of her previous year—especially her relationships with parents and relatives—will give her the opportunity to learn a number of important social and motor skills.

As her world expands beyond the boundaries of home and family life, she can apply everything she has learned about her parents, siblings, and other relatives to new encounters. This is particularly useful when it comes to her interacting with peers, as well as older or younger children. Her improved motor coordination will also allow her to toddle toward potential friends, hold out toys in an invitation to play, point toward interesting things, and "speak" to her new playmates, using various sounds or her own form of language. Children have a whole repertoire of interactions governing the way they relate to peers.

Making friends is a difficult process that doesn't always run smoothly.

At first, babies lack the skills of subtlety and social niceties, and may often appear aggressive, abrupt, or even mean to one another for no apparent reason. While your baby will have been studying social rules for many months by watching your reactions to her own behavior, as well as your responses to others, successfully applying these rules to a situation that finds her playing alongside another toddler will be a different endeavor. Unlike you, her peers may not react in the way she expects. Nor will she easily predict what will please or irritate them.

Early friendships are very much the product of each individual encounter. They may span only the length of a game and may need to be forged anew at the next meeting. Indeed, it is

RAISING A SOCIABLE BABY

Like older children and adults, some babies are better at making friends than others. There are many ways in which you can help the process along. Give your baby as many opportunities as possible to meet different people, and especially peers, right from the beginning. In day-to-day life, encourage interaction with friends and visitors, even people you meet in the street or a store. Your child will also carefully watch and learn from your own interaction with others, so be aware at all times that you are her social role model. Be there to reassure her when she is in the presence of a new person. Join parent and baby groups or music or swimming lessons in your area, and visit local playgrounds. These provide your baby with the perfect opportunity to expand her social network in a safe and comforting environment. Small, informal groups are good preparation for nursery, too, where your child will be faced with much larger groups of children and teachers in a more formal setting. Finally, while she learns to play with her peers, you should respond to your child's activities with loads of encouragement. Unless she turns to you for help, don't interfere, even if you see her getting into difficulty. It is important for her to have the space to make mistakes and social blunders from which she can learn about the world of people.

often the child with the best toy on the day who will be chosen as the "friend," leaving last week's best buddy forgotten. A child's world is filled with so many new people and experiences that the value of a particular friendship cannot yet be put into perspective. A new encounter, even with a familiar person, still requires building up a new strategy of interactive behavior.

Faced with a room full of potential new friends, your toddler will try a number of different tactics to enter an established game. She may attempt a nonverbal approach—hovering on the outskirts of the group and either waiting for an indication that she has been accepted or joining in gradually without upsetting the activities of her peers. Or she may opt for parallel play. This involves mimicking the actions and sounds already going on, in the hope that she will become amalgamated into the ongoing game.

When your child is somewhat older, she may try a more direct tactic, introducing her presence and offering herself as a new participant, expressing ideas and trying to make an impact from the start. This may not always go to plan. Alternatively, having learned from past mistakes, she may opt for a more gentle approach, asking for permission to join in with the well-worn phrase: "Can I play, too?"

Unfortunately, these approaches will not always be successful, and rejection can be upsetting to your child. Therefore, it is important for you to help your toddler in the new task of making friends; gentle encouragement can go a long way.

THE ASSERTIVE TODDLER

"Me do it!" After months of being carried around, wheeled about, and strapped into chairs, it isn't surprising that your toddler appears willful and demonstrates a growing desire for independence.

Becoming assertive has its roots in early infancy, when your baby gradually progresses from reflex-driven behavior to increasingly controlled, voluntary actions. These developments—which include controlling facial expressions, moving the arms and hands to reach or point, and producing increasingly complex vocalizations—lead to the specialization of various brain areas and allow for your baby to influence her environment and the people in it.

You should interpret your child's drive for self-assertion as a positive expression of flourishing independence and knowledge of the world.

Without a good understanding of the rules of social life and her place within her family and among her peers, your little one won't have the confidence, ability, or drive to express her desires and opinions. It is precisely because she will have had a solid, secure, and nurturing introduction to the social world that she will be ready to make her mark on it.

One of the first indications of the strong impulse for independence is when your toddler becomes a stickler for rules. Your two year old will fixate on certain routines and rules she has learned

Willing and able *to do things for himself, your toddler's efforts to be self assertive should be applauded instead of stifled.*

through observation. She gradually forms concepts about the way things should be and will get upset and even angry if, for example, her toys are put away in the wrong box or her favorite plastic duck is missing at bath time. This period is often referred to as "the terrible twos," because toddlers suddenly start throwing unexplainable tantrums about the most minor things. Having been so easy to please up to now, your toddler may suddenly grow increasingly demanding and bad-tempered.

Social referencing *occurs when your toddler checks your reactions before proceeding with an action.*

This is a time for you to adhere to all her routines whenever possible, however petty and arbitrary they may seem. It's also a time for a lot of patience. You can take heart from the knowledge that this is a relatively short-lived phase in your child's development, although you may need to brace yourself for the ride—the terrible twos often grow into the even more obstinate threes.

The onset of self-assertion is often accompanied by an increase in the use of "social referencing." This is when your toddler checks your reactions to a new experience or stimulus before deciding how to respond to it herself. So if father and child encounter a large dog in the street, she will look up at dad's face and gauge his response to know whether to be scared of the dog or whether to approach and pet it.

These behavioral developments seem to contradict each other, but by behaving in seemingly contradictory ways, your toddler achieves a crucial balance between being daringly independent and cleverly cautious. This willful phase can be difficult for both parents and children but it is a necessary and useful part of development, during which your toddler learns to manage her own behavior in the light of her growing knowledge of others. You must deal with it in a smart way and patiently if your child is to emerge confident and strengthened in her own independence, yet still respectful of the needs and wishes of others.

Managing the "terrible" twos and threes

A toddler behaving badly is just testing boundaries. These include the limits of your patience, the limits of the rules you set, and also, importantly, the limits of her own ability to impact on the world around her. By trying your patience, by acting against your wishes, by insisting on doing things her way, your child is actively pushing situations in different directions to discover what happens when things and situations are not as they should be. It is a form of trial and error, problem solving of a particularly exhausting kind.

Often, the best way of dealing with your toddler's frustrating demands is to purposely give in and let her find out that her wants are inappropriate and a

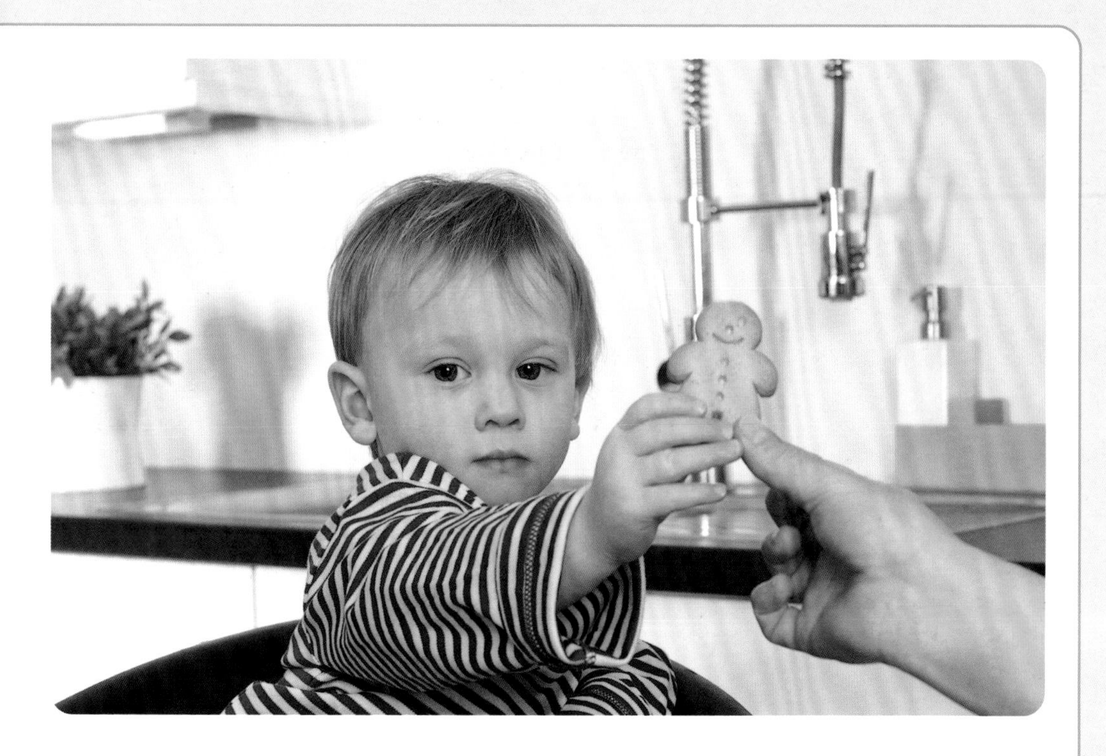

Distraction *instead of confrontation is normally the best strategy to adopt when dealing with conflict.*

detriment to herself. So, for instance, if she insists on wearing her favorite woollen pullover on a hot summer's day, let her. She will soon find it uncomfortable and sweaty, and take it off of her own accord. Give her a chance to learn from her mistakes. This is the only way the rules she has learned, and is inappropriately testing in this situation, will be altered to suit a new context.

There are obviously times when letting your child make her own decisions is impossible or even dangerous. When this is the case, keeping your cool and simply physically removing your child from the situation works best—even if it is accompanied by screams of protest. The best tactic in such situations is distraction. Whatever you do, don't get involved in an argument with your toddler. Remember, you are the adult, and there is nothing to be gained from your being proved right. Find something new and interesting to change your child's focus and put the incident behind you both as quickly as possible. Wait until a calmer moment to show her the error of her ways. You will have far more success teaching her the right way to behave in a positive situation when all is going well than when in the throws of a tear-filled moment.

3

How your baby learns to communicate

THE FASCINATING JOURNEY TO LANGUAGE

At just a few months old, and long before he is ready to produce his first words, your baby already manages to convey many of his feelings and desires. He can even share some of the things that he notices or finds interesting in his environment. Interaction takes many forms—words are just one of them. By using eye gaze and pointing, he can draw others' attention to objects or events, involving those around him in situations that capture his attention. By crying when he is unhappy, or by smiling, gurgling, or babbling when not, your little one can start to share his feelings and needs with you. Luckily for him, older children and adults instinctively respond to a baby's noises and efforts to establish joint attention by talking to him; they naturally comment on situations, filling in a baby's missing words or sentences, and they do so in a special way.

Next time you find yourself talking to your baby, notice the change in your intonation, in the words you choose, and in the way you deliver them. This is called "motherese"—a particular way of speaking that people naturally use when addressing young listeners. The term implies that it's a quality of speech belonging to only mothers. However, we all do it: mothers, fathers, men, women, and children. Even toddlers as young as three will alter the way they talk when they are chatting to someone clearly younger than themselves (see also page 64).

Your baby spends much of his time listening to the conversations going on around him, absorbing all kinds of information about language. While he gets more stimulation from speech actually addressed to him, new research has shown that he also pays some attention to conversations that go on between adults, so he learns from those, too.

Prior to developing enough cerebral maturity or sufficient control over his vocal apparatus to speak, your baby already feels a strong urge to communicate—being a resourceful little character, he'll find other means of "talking" to you. Crying, for instance, can have diverse acoustic properties. Without even having to try, you quickly learn to identify one cry to mean hunger, another to mean pain or discomfort, and yet another to say, "I'm bored" or "I want a hug".

Even once he is producing recognizable words, your little one will accompany them with plenty of gestures and eye movements to enhance his efforts to be understood.

The steps to language acquisition

In acquiring language, your baby has to learn to both understand and then produce the words he hears. These two facets of language start in early infancy—well before he utters anything recognizable. Early on, cooing, laughing, and other similar sounds are signs that your baby is trying out his articulatory system. Essential to the acquistition of speech, however, is the ability to hear, and all babies are given a hearing checkup within weeks of birth (see page 134).

Toward the middle of his first year, he will start using a series of language-like noises known as "babbling." At first, it may seem as if he were multilingual, producing sounds that are not part of his mother tongue, but gradually, at about nine months of age, his babbling will be reduced to the sounds particular to the language he hears around him.

Infants possess an ability that adults do not; until their brains become specialized to reflect their native tongues, they are able to distinguish a vast range of speech sounds belonging to other languages.

Your baby will probably begin producing recognizable words between his first and second birthdays. This step will probably be followed by a period of relatively slow progress, when he will produce only a handful of single words. Then there will be a sudden increase in the rapidity with which he starts to acquire and use new words. This is known as the "naming explosion"—a time when your baby can learn to produce as many as eight new words a day.

However, language is not only about words. Your child also has to learn about grammar: how to combine all the words he is learning to make meaningful dialogue. Each language has a grammar that regulates how words are put together and sentences are punctuated. In English, for instance, "Paul hit Peter" does not mean the same thing as "Peter hit Paul." In other languages, however, where different rules apply and special endings are added to names to indicate who does what to whom, word order plays a different role in highlighting what's important to the speaker.

Language also incorporates a level of what are called "paralinguistic clues," such as stress and intonation, which help you to determine whether you are being asked a question, ordered to do something, or are merely being told about an interesting fact. You also pick up clues from faces and bodies, not just voices. So if you cannot hear a voice because of background noise, you can lip-read and look at gestures to ascertain what the person is saying.

As an adult, you take for granted your ability to pick up on and combine all these aspects of communication. For your little one, however, these complex and tightly related levels of language are things that he will have to decipher and learn to use over his first years of life. Luckily for him, he will get a lot of help from others during his journey to language acquisition, so that by the time your child approaches his fourth birthday, he will have become a fluent speaker who can take talking for granted. Following this, he will then be ready to embark on the exciting road to reading.

Communicating without words

Crying is the most effective means of communication available to young infants. Although it is one of a range of vocalizations that your baby will make during his first six months of life, it is by far the most common and frequent.

Your baby cries in response to specific physiological and emotional states, such as discomfort, pain, boredom, fear, loneliness, hunger, or the need to be changed. Even his first cry in the delivery room had an important communicative role. It signaled to the doctor or midwife that his lungs had successfully filled with air and it evoked strong emotions in you, his new parents.

The nature of early cries can also indicate the presence of problems, such as respiratory difficulties, which professionals may use as indices for assessing the baby's central nervous system.

A vocabulary of tears

Your baby's cries are unique to him. Much like fingerprints, they have their own distinctive intonation, pitch, rhythm, and intensity.

Differences in crying sounds are produced by regulating the amount of air being forced through the vocal cords and by varying the patterns of pauses and loudness. It is this individual quality of a baby's cries that makes it possible for you to recognize the unique sound of your own baby.

Recordings of babies' cries have demonstrated that they can range across five octaves in pitch. Even more amazing is that crying is influenced by a child's mother tongue. New research shows that French babies' cries have a rising melodic contour compared to German babies' cries, which tend to be characterized by a falling contour.

Within a few weeks of birth, you will have begun to distinguish between your baby's different cries, knowing from the varying sounds whether he is hungry, overtired, or seems to need a clean diaper (see the box, opposite). Crying is such a successful means of communication that siblings as young as seven can "read" the meaning of their baby brother's or sister's cries. Interestingly, newborns also seem to pay particular attention to the special sound of crying: especially young infants often start crying themselves when they hear another baby wailing nearby. This is not imitation. Instead, it is a response to the physiological effect that this particularly arresting noise has on young children. In fact, researchers have found that babies are so intrigued by the sounds that accompany tears that if their own cries are recorded and played back to them during a tearful moment, they will stop crying almost instantly to attend and respond to the sound.

Your physical responses to crying

Although you are probably acutely aware of your emotional responses to your baby's cries—be it anxiety, sadness, frustration, or even anger—you may be less conscious of the physiological reactions going on inside your own body. You probably know from experience that the sound can stimulate your breast glands to produce milk, if you are breastfeeding, but did you realize that hearing your little one cry can cause a rise in your blood pressure and can speed up your heart-rate?

It has been found that the level of physiological changes (such as how much faster your heart will beat or how much higher your blood pressure will rise) can actually differ as a function of the meaning of each type of cry. This may explain why parents often rate the effect of hearing their baby's tears of hunger or pain as considerably more stressful and upsetting than cries of boredom or tiredness, which tend to be more restrained.

In reaction to your infant's range of cries, you will develop a repertoire of responses, including feeding, picking up, cuddling, talking, changing diapers, and, usually when your baby has been put to bed, a wait-and-see-if-baby-will-stop-by-himself response.

MORE ABOUT **THE CRYING CODE**

To those who don't have children of their own, the idea that parents can tell what is wrong with their baby based on the sound of the cry may seem dubious. However, the secret lies in listening to the clues given by the baby himself, because each baby has a repertoire of different cries signaling specific needs.

Studies have shown that the hunger cry is generally rhythmic, with a braying quality, often accompanied by repetitive movements, such as kicking or twisting. In contrast, cries of boredom are less regular and coordinated, and may have longer pauses as a baby stops and waits to look or listen out for the desired response. Cries of pain, on the other hand, are much more intense and high-pitched, signaling urgency to the listener. These may be accompanied by reddening of the baby's face, arching of his back, and general muscle contractions as he tenses in response to the discomfort.

Crying can vary in other ways, too. With the onset of babbling, for instance, your baby will test out an increasingly large range of phonetic sounds, and you may start to distinguish distinct vowel sounds in his cries of protest as he attempts to inject even more meaning into this early method of communication.

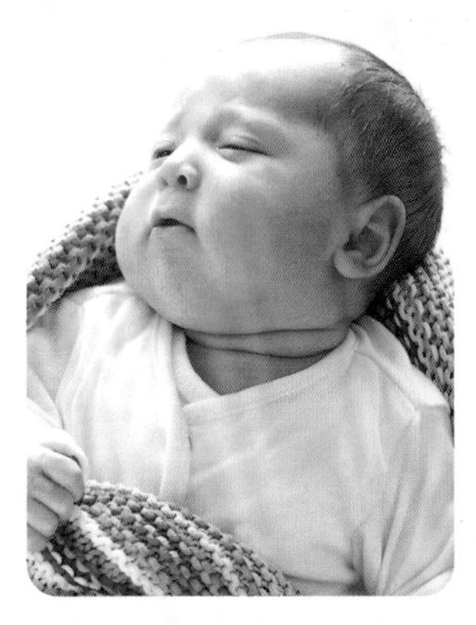

Responding to your baby

Physical comfort (picking up your baby and holding or rocking him) will usually be the most successful initial response to crying. However, if your baby is not signaling that he is hungry or needs changing, then auditory stimulation, such as talking to him or playing music, will often work. During his first few weeks of life, your baby may find white noise (such as the sound of an untuned television or radio channel or the rhythmic noise from a washing machine or car engine) soothing, especially when accompanied by repetitive motion. This is why, when your baby is being particularly fractious, drives in the car or walks in a stroller or sling may have such magical effects. However, try not to get in the habit of always resorting to such drastic measures. There are times when letting your baby cry it out may be unavoidable—say, if you are in the middle of trying to establish a good sleeping routine. Setting up a workable daily schedule, adhering to regular bedtimes, and using calming distractions, such as music to listen to, or mobiles to watch, will help to keep tears at bay.

You face an added challenge when it comes to childhood tears—the nature of crying progressively changes as a function of your baby's age and development. The set of responses or soothing strategies that may have worked wonders during his first few weeks may become redundant as your baby matures. You can spend weeks learning to recognize different cries, only for them to change as soon as you crack the code.

Regardless of how old your baby is, acting on a cry is always better than ignoring it. It is a mistake to believe that reacting too eagerly to crying will produce a spoiled, manipulative child. Research has shown time and again that failing to respond to crying often causes a baby to become even more distressed, and, as a result, he will simply intensify his cry. Keep in mind that in the early months of life, your infant has no other means of successfully communicating with you. If you choose to ignore his cries, all he can do is try harder and cry louder. In fact, young babies whose cries are answered quickly have been found to be more secure and strongly attached to their parents as a result. Furthermore, they develop and learn to use more varied types of noncrying communication at an earlier age than those whose cries have not been responded to promptly. Far from reinforcing a negative behavior, by responding sensitively and consistently to your baby's cries, you are telling him that he has successfully communicated with you and that you can always be relied on to respond to his needs.

Physical comfort, *which will normally be your initial response, can take the form of holding your baby close and caressing him or rocking him in your arms.*

Communicating negativity

When your baby averts his gaze, shrinks away from your touch, cries, or fusses in response to the attention you give him, he is communicating his displeasure in the only way he knows how. It is neither an expression of rejection nor evidence that your bond with him is threatened. Far from it, it is, in fact, a positive sign that your baby is actively striving to make a mark on the world. Expressing negativity is part of normal interaction; it is one of the many communicative tools with which your baby can control his social and physical environments to fit his needs.

In the first weeks

Scientists used to believe that negative behavior emerged at around six months when it was thought that a baby was able to translate his feelings into voluntary actions. More recently, however, research has shown that negativity can be identified in infants as young as two or three weeks of age. Young babies seem regularly to alternate between positive and negative responses in their everyday interactions with parents, siblings, or carers. Crying is the most obvious and common form of negativity; it is used to maintain a stable environment and to ensure the provision of food, care, and comfort. The same is true of fussing.

Fussing is often interpreted as a sign of "bad temper," or as proof that a baby is "difficult" or "demanding," whereas, in fact, he may be attempting to communicate negative reactions to some specific event.

Expressing negativity without crying

Apart from crying, your baby can exhibit many other, more subtle forms of negativity, including:

- Changing position to distance himself from another person.
- Turning his head away.
- Arching or stiffening his back.
- Refusing to return smiles or to establish eye contact.
- Handling clothes or blankets excessively.
- Touching his own face repeatedly.
- Sucking his thumb or fingers.
- Pushing a person away with his hands or feet.

Your baby may use all of these behaviors to convey his negative feelings toward a situation in which he finds himself.

There is disagreement on what causes negative responses. Some scientists have suggested that negativity occurs when a baby is faced with "perceptual overload." In other words, when a situation is overstimulating—too much is happening at once for a baby to cope with. In this situation, his senses become overly heightened and he will respond by withdrawing or rejecting. While it is, indeed, the case that babies can sometimes be overwhelmed by a particular experience, experiments have shown that this does not account for negativity in general. Researchers have demonstrated that it is the quality, not simply the quantity, of stimulation that influences whether a baby's responses will be positive or negative (see the box, page 60).

Interestingly, "negative" reactions usually do not occur in situations where mother–child interaction is more naturally interrupted. For example, if you were in the middle of playing with your baby and a friend were to walk in and interrupt, causing you to stop looking at and responding to your infant for a while, your little one would not find this surprising and, therefore, would not automatically respond negatively. So from an espeically young age, your baby is already sensitive to some of the special rules of social interaction. Negativity is more often than not caused by the frustration your baby feels when his expectations are violated. If his environment becomes incomprehensible, he will probably respond by first withdrawing, then becoming distracted, and, finally, by rejecting the stimulus altogether. He may also react negatively when he finds himself incapable of conveying his desires correctly, such as when experiencing discomfort or tiredness and not being able convey this to you. What is also interesting is that uncommunicative behavior—when your baby doesn't respond to stimulation as expected—will often be naturally interpreted by you as "negative." One study found that during observations of mother–baby interactions in a natural setting, up to 20 percent of a baby's movements or gestures were interpreted as negative by the parent. Common remarks made by mothers included: "You're tired of this game, aren't you?" or "You don't want to smile at mommy, do you?" This tendency to interpret your infant's lack of response as negative is probably due to the fact that when he fusses, withdraws, or loses interest, you will naturally feel a sense of rejection or inadequacy.

This, in turn, can affect the way you then communicate back to your child, which may only exacerbate the negativity. So, the next time your baby seems grumpy or refuses your invitation to interact, remind yourself that he is not being negative; he may simply be expressing himself and trying to communicate something that in all likelihood has nothing to do with your attempts to engage with him.

MORE ABOUT

TESTING NEGATIVITY IN YOUNG BABIES

In one particular experiment on infant negativity, two-month-old babies were encouraged to watch and respond to video images of their mothers. Each baby was seated in front of a screen with the researcher, while his mother was hidden from view and videotaped. Each mother was able to see her baby's reactions clearly, and was asked to either respond appropriately or inappropriately to them. In the first instance, the mother reacted appropriately to her baby's changing facial expressions, vocalizations, and gestures, and the baby was able to see this on screen. In the second trial, the mother was asked to respond inappropriately or not at all to her baby's interaction. Results showed that when the babies' expectations of maternal behavior were violated—for example, when a mother continued looking at her baby but frowned in response to his smile—the infants displayed negative behavior; they turned away from the video image and looked puzzled or frowned. They would yawn, fiddle with clothes, and touch their own faces, and then, as they grew increasingly frustrated, they would begin fussing to clearly express displeasure.

Learning to smile

Long before he is able to control his facial muscles, a baby's lips pull back to form a smiling shape. Scans have revealed that even in the uterus life, fluctuations in the fetal central nervous systems cause the corners of babies' mouths to upturn slightly. One- and two-week-old babies may make similar mouth movements in response to loud sounds or voices, or even in their sleep—giving the impression to those who witness such "smiles" that the infants are communicating positivity or experiencing pleasant dreams. At this stage, however, a smiling mouth simply represents an automatic muscular response to stimulation, involving only the muscles in the lower face. Interestingly, girl infants display this spontaneous smiling reflex twice as often as boys, whereas boys have a much stronger startle reflex. The reflex "smile" is elicited by both human and nonhuman sounds. Only later will it become a selective reaction to specific pleasurable experiences and emotions.

The involuntary grin

By his third week of life, your infant will be capable of a grinlike expression, usually in response to sounds—mainly voices—when he is in an alert and attentive state. However, he is not yet responding in a truly social way, because at this stage, his facial expression is still an involuntary reflex to stimulation. Yet, it prompts you to grin back enthusiastically every time it happens, thereby promoting interaction and closeness between you and your child. The involuntary grin, therefore, actually has an important purpose in social development. Also, by engaging his muscles in these frequent responses, your baby will gain control over his facial expressions, and your enthusiastic reaction encourages him to repeat the expression. Gradually, he will learn how to produce these "smiles" in a more voluntary fashion, so that by four weeks of age, his smile is no longer just a physical reflex, but an intended response. However, even with this new ability to grin at will, your little one's smiles are not what we call "social smiles," because he will still probably grin at both an inanimate object and a person, or smile in response to both negative and positive situations.

The first voluntary smiles

Once he masters the mechanics of voluntary smiling, your baby will begin using it increasingly frequently, which helps him to gain a better understanding of the meaning of smiling. From the age of five or six weeks onward, he will smile at almost anything that captures his attention. The grin will become a major part of your young baby's repertoire of interactions, and although its social purpose still remains something of a mystery to him, he soon learns to associate the action with the positive attention it brings.

At around eight weeks of age, your baby will begin to

smile more selectively in response to only certain things or situations, such as a particular toy, noise or action by you. He now also begins to show a distinct preference for smiling at people instead of objects. This development indicates the end of the reflex-driven smile. At this age, however, your baby still doesn't really know what smiling is all about. When coming across varying tones of voice or facial expressions, he may still smile at an angry face or irritable voice. So when your young baby smiles back at you, he may be smiling in response to the change in your mouth shape and not necessarily to the emotions that your facial expression conveys.

The social smile

The first truly "social smiles" will emerge at around four months of age. Now, your baby will grin in response to other people's smiles or laughter. He will have discovered what smiling really means:—it is an exchange of information that conveys gladness. He will understand that you are contented and smile back to tell you that he feels the same. Alternatively, he may initiate interaction by smiling at you to encourage you to pay him more attention.

Soon, your baby will learn to use different types of smiles, too—with closed lips, or bared teeth, or an open mouth—to communicate different moods. He will carefully monitor your varying reactions to his repertoire of grins. Studies have shown that adults generally respond to all types of baby grins by smiling back. However, one particular type—when baby smiles with bared teeth—tends to encourage an adult not only to smile back but to vocalize and nod as well or even laugh.

So for babies especially, smiles are indeed worth a thousand words.

The laughter factor

Your baby will start laughing a few weeks after his social smile emerges. Although you may notice him making laughing-type vocalizations as early as three months of age, at this stage he is only testing sounds and responses. He will not necessarily "laugh" at the same thing on different occasions, because laughter has not yet become a selective response. Something that really amuses him one day may fail to bring even a smile the next. This isn't due to the fact that putting on a silly hat, singing a funny song, or miming with a toy has become boring to your baby. It is simply that he cannot yet select laughter as a voluntary response to communicate his enjoyment or excitement. The most fail-safe way to prompt laughter in your young baby is through auditory and tactile stimulation, such as funny sounds and tickling. Later, as laughing becomes a regular part of his interactions with others, watching something amusing, or playing games that contain an element of surprise, such as peekaboo, will reliably elicit laughter, too.

The "purpose" of laughing

Laughter, like smiling, fulfills an important social function. Primarily, it encourages ongoing exchanges between your baby and others but, more than that, it ensures that whatever caused the laughter in the first place will be repeated by the person in charge of the interaction. This natural propensity for repetition in parent–child interaction is crucial, because it gives your baby several opportunities to learn about, make sense of, and anticipate each experience. By repeating an enjoyable game, sound, or activity several times over, you let your little one form a clear memory of it from which he can then make predictions not only about your behavior, but his as well. By laughing and smiling in response to certain games and not others, he is also able to place important limits on the ways in which you entertain him. So, in effect, it is your baby more than you who actively sets the agenda for the fun and games in which you both take part.

Your child's use of smiles and laughter will change as he matures.

When he is older and already well versed in the social smile, he will still, at times, use the facial expression inappropriately, especially in situations that make him feel unsure. Your baby will often smile or laugh in response to unfamiliar or even scary things; this is his first impulse, as he attempts to make sense of what he is experiencing. However, this smile can quickly turn into a cry. For instance, if you place a mask in front of your face, your baby may initially find it amusing, but once he realizes that it has replaced the face he knows and expects to see, he will become unsure and start to cry.

The more arousing a stimulus, the more probable it will elicit laughter, as long as your baby does not perceive it as dangerous. Your baby might be fascinated by a flickering flame, for instance, but he will not smile at it because he can sense a threat of true danger there.

Responding to your actions

Your baby may only smile and laugh once he has assessed your reactions to something. This is an important function known as "social referencing." It means that your baby is starting to use your responses to things to gauge what his should be, and he will sometimes only find something amusing after your laughter has assured him that it is. So you should make the most of this phase; laughing at your own jokes and convincing your little one that you are the most accomplished of entertainers may never be that easy again.

Talking to your baby

Adults instinctively adjust the way they speak when addressing babies or especially young children. This style of speech is usually referred to as "motherese" (see also page 54), although the term "parentese" would be more accurate, because—as you've seen—moms and dads all tend to speak like that to babies.

Multifunctional "motherese"

"Motherese" is an automatic response that prompts a person to:

- Alter the pitch of his or her voice.
- Enunciate words more clearly.
- Opt for simple, clear grammar.

It is something people often do unconsciously—not just when talking to young children and babies, but also sometimes instinctively when addressing foreigners or people with hearing impairments. This predisposition to adapt the way we speak when interacting with someone less linguistically able than ourselves is smart, because it ensures that the language the listener hears is best suited for the task of learning.

Although "motherese" is not designed to act as an actual teaching tool for words and grammar, it does promote sustained attention between you and your baby within the context of language. By using this way of speaking, you

are able to hold your child's attention for longer periods, and, therefore, increase the chances of being properly heard and understood.

"Motherese" has several unique characteristics that differentiate it from normal speech. Most noticeably, it tends to be high-pitched and uses a much wider range of intonation patterns, often including a rising tone at the end of each sentence; in normal adult speech, your tone will usually tend to fall at the close of sentences.

A rising tone is far more captivating to the ear and it is this, combined with marked rhythms and a regulated speed of delivery, that gives motherese its sing-song quality.

Having naturally adapted the sound of your voice to grab your baby's attention, you then sustain it by making use of certain "tricks" that you instinctively know will keep your young listener interested—you:

- Maintain eye contact.
- Use his name frequently.
- Include many questions, prompts, and explanatory hand gestures.
- Engage in regular physical contact all the while.

Until he is able to use language well, you will automatically choose to concentrate on things that can be seen, heard, pointed at, or felt. In other words, situations that can be referred to in the immediate: "Look at that doggie! Isn't it a nice doggie?" You will use short, simple sentences; repeat nouns, and avoid pronouns, so that your speech is relatively slow and rhythmic with plenty of repetition. Because motherese generally only refers to the here and now, you are, for instance, unlikely to say to your baby: "Wasn't that a nice doggie? Did you like the doggie we met yesterday?," because you know that these words alone are not enough to convey meaning or sustain your baby's interest at this early stage.

As well as maintaining attention, "motherese" is also the means by which you can expand your child's utterances naturally, without implying error or setting up a teacher–pupil dynamic. By using this form of speech, you gently add to the things your child says to you in a way that isn't intrusive and which, therefore, continues to bolster his growing use of language. So, for instance, if your toddler says to you: "Cat!," you will not simply look to where he is pointing, you will instinctively start a dialogue by incorporating his word into a longer sentence, usually ending in a question. For example, "Oh yes, there's a cat! A nice white cat! Shall we go and see the cat?" This not only ensures that your baby is drawn into a two-way exchange, but also renders the interaction as conversation-like as possible.

Altering your speech when talking to your infant is instinctive. In return, your baby shows a distinct preference for listening to "motherese" over normal speech. Then, as your baby matures, you (and other speakers) will automatically adjust the way you talk and what you say to reflect his changing level of comprehension. Sentences will grow in length, grammar will gain layers, new words will be continually introduced, and learning will be reinforced. Ultimately, what motherese does during the early months is to encourage your baby to pay special attention, to and engage in, language-based interaction.

Research has shown that altering one's speech when talking to infants is such a strong human drive that, within only days of birth, parents already adapt the way they speak when addressing their baby.

Dialogues of a different kind

As already discussed, communication is not completely about talking or even vocalizing. Dialogues between parents and babies start well before infants begin to understand or produce real language. Research has shown that if four-month-old infants are shown two faces, one mouthing the sound "ee" and the other the sound "oo," they will look longer at the face that corresponds with the sound heard through a loudspeaker. In other words, from early on, they can already match specific mouth shapes to specific speech sounds. In fact, infants are so sensitive to this that they show distress if the sounds produced by the parent on a television monitor are not simultaneous with the movements of the parent's mouth. Studies also show that infants gradually learn to expect certain specific words from their parents in response to specific situations. This hails the beginning of mapping words onto objects or events.

"Conversations" without words

Even without words, two-way communication between adults and infants is important, because it shares many qualities relevant to language. For instance, as a result of nonverbal interaction, babies early on become aware of the pattern

HOW *you can help*

As a parent, you should take every opportunity to interact with your baby. The more experience he has in turn-taking exchanges, the better equipped he will be for future language acquisition. However silly you might feel chatting to yourself in public, talk to your baby, whenever he is alert, about the things you see, hear, or feel, about thoughts you have, about anything and everything. Engaging with your child like this not only helps to develop communication

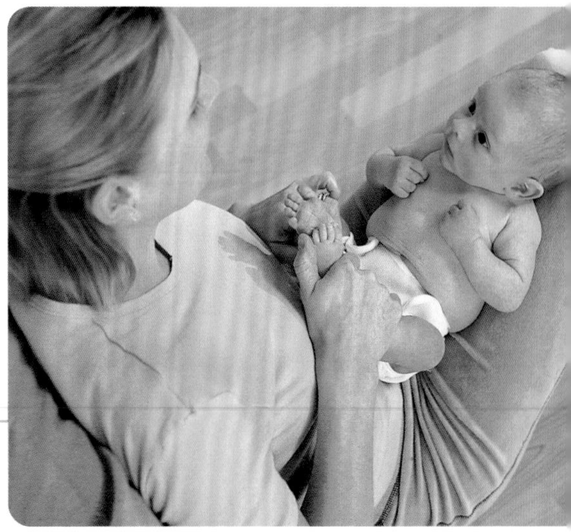

of taking turns in dialogue—in which one party is active while the other is quiet, and then the sequence is reversed. This pattern is found in almost all forms of interaction between parent and child, be it a game of peekaboo, a moment of joint attention, or "chatting" during a ritual such as when changing diapers or feeding. In these situations, there is a reciprocity between a baby and an adult whereby each will contribute to the exchange with peaks of activity, attention, and vocalization interspersed by quiet pauses. Each party pays close attention to the other's responses and reacts appropriately, or what psychologists call "contingently," and each turn is designed to keep the interaction going.

A baby may slowly build up his responses to a crescendo, then become quiet and wait to see how mom or dad responds. The parent, in turn, will react with increasing enthusiasm, mimicking the baby's facial expressions and respecting his turns, then instigating a new cycle of "dialogue" when the baby tires of the current one.

These early nonlinguistic "conversations" lay the foundations for later real dialogues using language. Indeed, prelinguistic dialogues can be so efficient that some parents have made use of whole "vocabularies" of hand gestures to converse with their infants before their baby's articulatory apparatus allows for the onset of language production.

COMMUNICATING WITH YOUR BABY

skills, it strengthens your bond and helps him to learn about his world.

Imitation games are a great way to encourage two-way interaction. You can try simple hiding of faces behind hands, clapping games, singing songs, or just making silly sounds to him. When you notice your little one paying attention to something, follow his gaze and add dialogue to the situation, naming the object, person, or action taking place, and generally filling in the language gaps wherever possible. Just because your baby doesn't yet understand every word you utter doesn't mean he isn't gaining a great deal from your monologues. Remember, children understand language long before they produce it, so it's never too early to fill your baby's world with words.

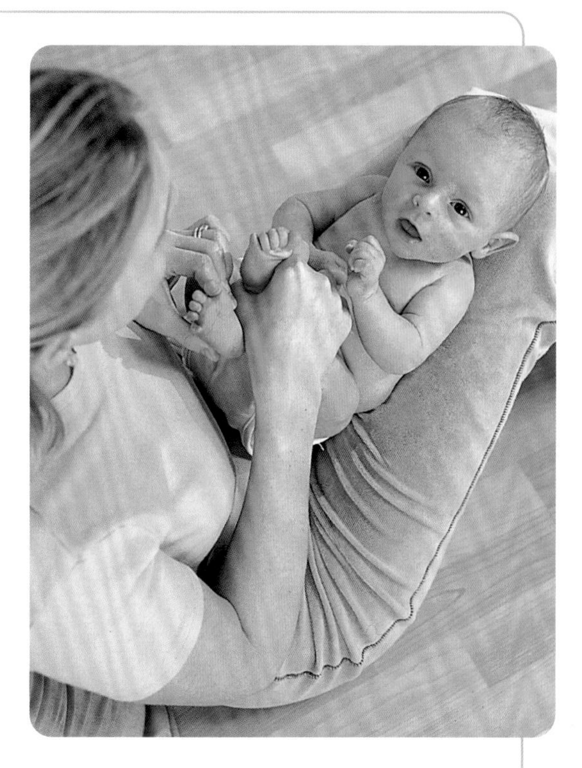

Talking fingers

Hand gestures allow for babies to exchange information with those around them. However, of all the different actions that your baby does with his fingers and thumbs—reaching, grasping, waving, clapping, and so on—pointing is by far the most communicative. It is a social action with two purposes: first, it enables your baby to get someone to give him something he wants but cannot reach, and second, and more important, it permits him to share interesting information. This latter function has been particularly proved in that it has been found that although babies may reach out with an extended arm to try and get something, they don't point at interesting events when alone. Nor will they bother pointing until they have first attracted someone's attention with eye gaze. Pointing, then, is truly communicative.

The varieties of pointing

Being able to point requires both motor dexterity and an understanding of certain basic rules of interaction and cause and effect, and this is why it takes a good six to nine months for this behavior to emerge.

Sometime in the second half of his first year, then, your baby will begin pointing to objects out of his reach to direct your attention to them. This form of pointing is called "instrumental pointing" and represents a specific and intentional means–end action. The resulting reaction from you—to pick up the toy and hand it to your baby—can be predicted and is generally confirmed. Within a few months, however, you may be perplexed by a new response when you go and get the coveted object your baby was pointing at. When you hand it over, he may look displeased, frown, or even push it away. Your little one is feeling

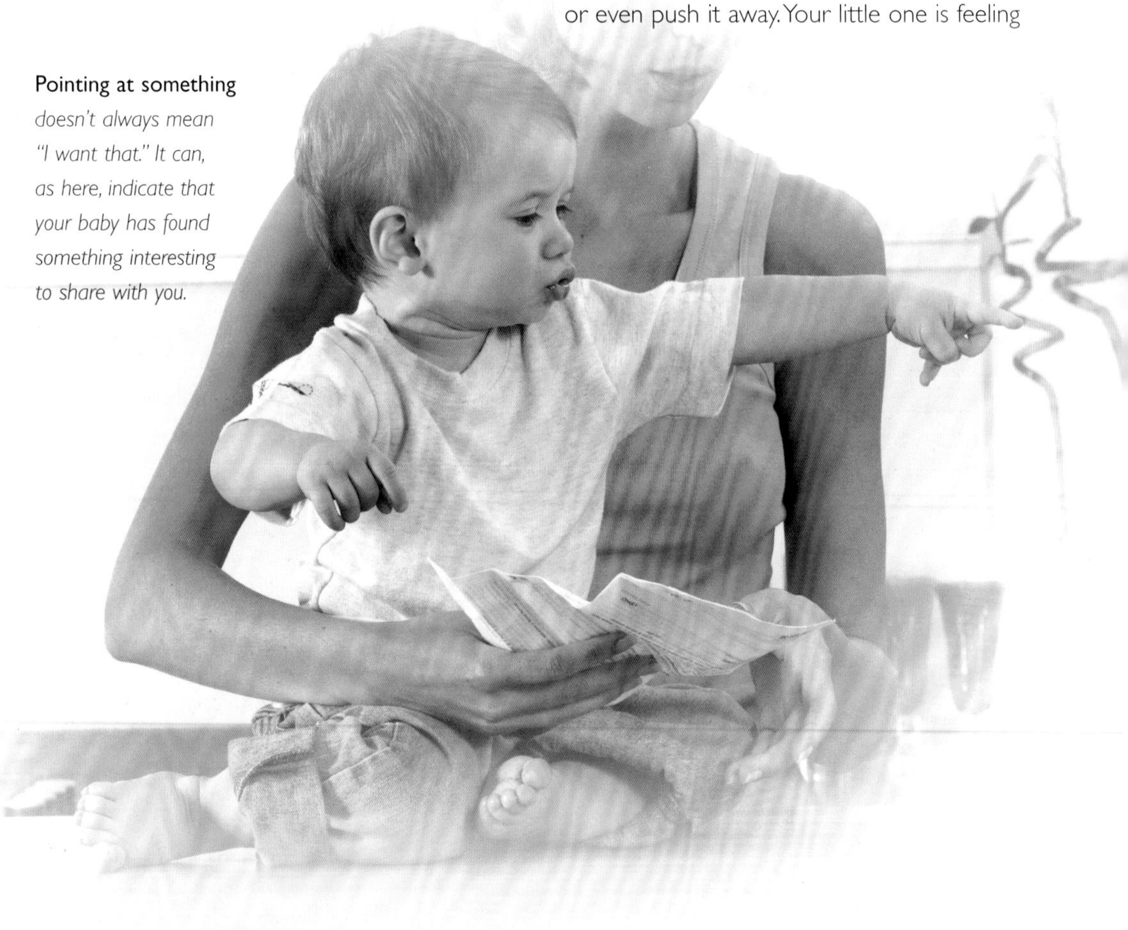

Pointing at something *doesn't always mean "I want that." It can, as here, indicate that your baby has found something interesting to share with you.*

frustrated. He didn't intend for you to get the object; he was pointing it out to share an experience with you. This form of pointing is called "declarative pointing." In this case, the finger gesture was not designed to convey, "See that object over there, please can you get it for me," but instead, "Look at that object, Mommy, isn't it interesting." No wonder your getting it has caused a frown.

Declarative pointing emerges toward the end of the first year of life and marks an important stage in development. Your baby's new endeavor to share experiences implies that he has grasped something fundamental about how beliefs and feelings are communicated. Attracting your attention by pointing to something is also his way of initiating dialogue and inviting you to interact. By pointing out a dog walking past in the street, your little one is not saying, "I want that dog, get it." Instead, he is encouraging you to join in with an experience that he is himself enjoying: "I like that dog, let's look at it together." So this special form of pointing enables your baby to communicate quite complex messages and prompt you to comment on the situation.

The use of declarative pointing is also a clue to language development. It usually precedes the onset of word use by just a few weeks and can act as an index of a baby's language comprehension. It not only enables your baby to respond to your object-naming games but also gives him the means to "ask" for new words to be supplied.

Through pointing and naming games, your baby learns that there is a word for everything to which he directs your attention.

When he finally starts uttering his first words, he will still regularly use pointing to complete a phrase. Therefore, although pointing is part of prelinguistic communication, it can also act as an integral part of early grammar learning—an invaluable communicative tool for your little one as he sets off on his journey to language use.

From babbling to talking

While still in the womb, your little one was already becoming familiar with the rise and fall, rhythms, and general patterns of speech—sounds that he will continue to find fascinating throughout his babyhood. Speech is the most common sound your infant listens to during his waking hours. However, without the necessary control over his own vocal apparatus, he cannot utter speech sounds of his own. This is why his earliest utterances, from around two or three months of age, are coos and cries, usually produced in response to your own vocalizations or directed at an object that has attracted his attention. These are produced at the back of the throat and involve only a few muscles. At this stage, your baby is simply learning to create

BORN TO SPEAK ANY LANGUAGE

It may surprise you to know that your baby was initially equipped with the ability to distinguish every one of the speech sounds that make up the 6,000 or so languages of the world. Language sounds are called "phonemes" and you may have come across the term "phonetics" in a preschool or early-years setting. Phonetics is an approach to reading education that focuses on the sounds that make up words. Every language is made up of a limited set of phonemes, and these are not the same across different tongues. This means that certain sound differentials, such as "l" and "r," for instance—which in English are obvious and mark the difference between unrelated words, such as "river" and "liver" or "rice" and "lice"—are in other tongues, such as Japanese, not distinguished. In Japanese, no word meanings are differentiated by "l" and "r" and to the Japanese ear the two sounds are the same. So, when a Japanese adult hears the English words "rice" and "lice," he or she does not detect the subtle change between them. However, the young Japanese baby would easily do so. This is because until his brain becomes specialized for the sounds of a particular language—at around nine or ten months when he is babbling his way to early word production in his mother tongue—a baby's hearing remains sensitive to all the speech sounds of the world, be they relevant to his own language or not.

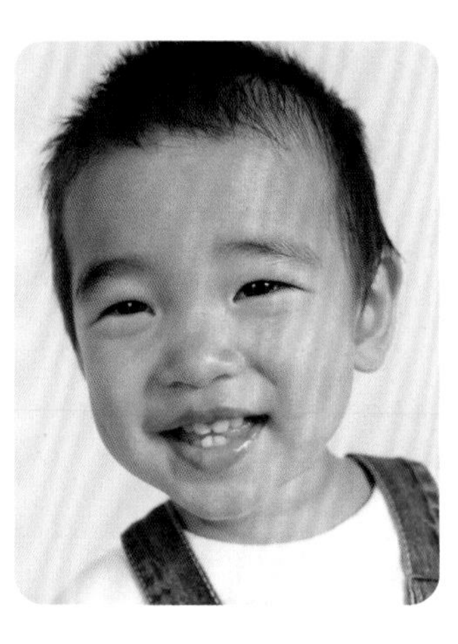

How do we know this? Because scientists have devised clever ways of testing what young babies are able to detect and/or find particularly stimulating in their environment. One of the methods used to study language development is called the "head-turning" technique. In these experiments, babies are placed in an infant seat with specially designed sounds at different pitches, testing out his vocal chords and lungs to see what they are capable of.

Decoding your baby's babbles

Between four and six months, however, the variety of vocalizations your baby will produce increases significantly as he discovers that using his mouth, tongue, and lips alters the sounds emitted from his throat. He will now begin to delight you with raspberry sounds (rough precursors to consonants) that he sometimes alternates with coos. This is called "marginal babbling," and represents your baby's first attempts at combining vowel and consonant-type sounds to produce more language-like utterances. Unsurprisingly, the easier a sound is to produce, the earlier it will appear in his babbling repertoire. This explains why some word sounds, such as "da," emerge earlier than others. However, that is not the whole story. Although your young infant was born with the ability to distinguish and eventually produce speech sounds from all human languages, from the time recognizable vowels and consonants

headphones that emit a repeated sound. At regular intervals, this sound is substituted by a new one, at which point a dancing toy appears to one side of the chair to mark the change. Babies quickly learn to anticipate the toy's appearance at each new sound, and turn their heads to look for it before it appears.

By using this method with different speech sounds, both from the baby's mother tongue and from foreign languages, scientists are able to discover which phonetic variations infants can or cannot detect. In Hindi, for instance, there are two different "da" sounds. To the adult English ear, these sound the same, but a six-month-old baby growing up in an English-speaking household would turn his head in response to this particular change, as would a Hindi baby at any age. However, by the time he is a year old, the English-speaking baby would not respond to each because his brain has by then become specialized for his native tongue.

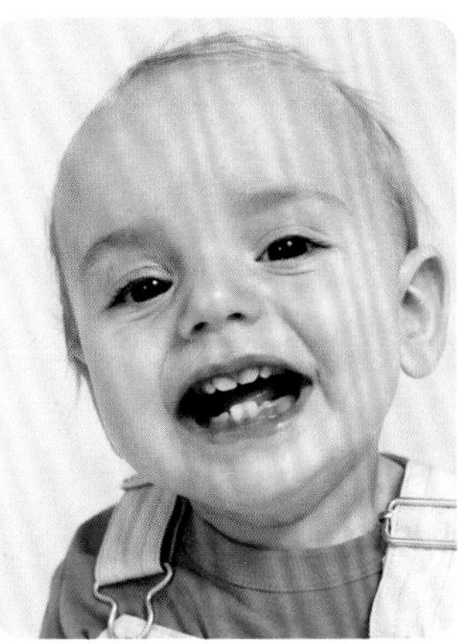

What these studies have shown is that up to the age of nine or ten months, babies retain the amazing capacity to distinguish the speech sounds of all languages, regardless of their mother tongue. This is one of the reasons why it is so easy and natural for young children to learn more than one language. However, toward the end of their first year, children begin to lose that ability. Having increasingly familiarized themselves with the primary language (or languages) spoken at home, they are no longer able to hear some of the more subtle phonetic variations of foreign tongues. So, by the time your toddler blows out the candle on his first birthday cake, his brain will be fine-tuned to the particular sounds of his mother tongue and his language comprehension will be well under way—he is geared up and ready to start talking.

are detected in your baby's babbling repertoire, processes in his brain start to change. Connections relating to foreign sounds will be weakened, while those pertinent to his mother tongue will be strengthened. In other words, sounds that do not belong to the language or languages he is learning will be produced less frequently, and those that he hears daily will begin to determine the way he babbles.

The next stage of babbling occurs at around nine to ten months and involves the use of clear syllabic utterances. Your baby is now able to produce strings of sounds that move smoothly from consonants to vowels. For you, as with many parents, this may feel like the start of "talking." What previously sounded like random sounds from your baby will now be replaced by wordlike strings, such as "da-da-da" or "mi-mi-mi"—vocalizations to which it is tempting to attribute meaning. Yet, at this stage, of course, such babbles have no referential value. They are still just sound games. Nevertheless, "canonical babbling," as this stage is known, represents an important step in language development. If carefully analyzed, the sound strings produced actually contain some basic rhythmic patterns of vocabulary as well as important tonal variation—all vital practice for later speaking.

Once that phase is mastered, your baby will begin experimenting with more complex sound strings: variegated sequences, such as "biba" or "tati." Now his utterances will sound noticeably different from the babbles of another infant learning a different language. Your soon-to-be-talking baby will be babbling in his mother tongue and nearing the end of the prelinguistic phase and is so accustomed to the sound of his own language (or languages, in the case of a multilingual child) that he will no longer be able to discriminate certain foreign speech sounds that he used to clearly distinguish. He may now embellish his "chatting" with gestures, facial expressions, and changes in his tone of voice, and you may also detect rising and falling patterns that mimic questions versus statements, as well as marked pauses during which your baby expects you to take your conversational turn. He's almost there.

Early word comprehension

At some point during the latter half of his first year, your baby will start to understand a limited set of words. This happens long before he is able to actually produce recognizable words himself, but the feedback he receives from his increasingly language-like babbles is invaluable to later speech development. It provides constant encouragement and clear models for actual word production. Because, although babbles do not carry meaning, you (and other adults) will often respond to them as if they do, listening, smiling, nodding, and joining in. You should often similar-sounding words in response, or copy your baby's babbles to start dialogues that incorporate his utterances as if they were real words. Through this feedback cycle, your baby is able to gradually replace his babbles with increasingly wordlike sounds until he perfects these to form distinguishable meaningful words.

First words

Most babies produce their first conventional words sometime between the ages of 10 and 20 months. However, unlike certain other milestones, such as sitting or becoming mobile, being able to produce recognizable words does not necessarily indicate that a child is an "early" or "late" developer. Comprehension is just as important—even if a baby is not actually saying anything.

From eight months of age onward, your baby will have been learning the meanings of new words on a daily basis. Whether he decides to try to vocalize the words in his growing vocabulary is dependent not only on his level of development, but on many other factors, such as temperament, family life, the presence of siblings, nursery experience, and so on. The important thing to remember is that his ability to understand language progresses at a considerably faster rate than language production. It is also worth noting that early words are often hard to tell apart from babbles, especially once the latter become more complex and varied.

A baby's first words tend to refer to objects or experiences with which he is most familiar. For instance: favorite people ("mama," "dada," his name, or that of his sibling), common objects ("car," "juice," "milk," "teddy"), and common words that adults use often, such as "no," "more," or "bye-bye." You will naturally react to your baby's attempts at producing words by repeating and renaming objects in different sentence contexts. This varied reinforcement will not only prompt your child to try again but also provides a consistent model of language.

Hearing your baby talk for the first time is a magical moment.

Your baby's first words

The first time your baby speaks can be a fleeting moment or one that may not recur as soon or as often as you might expect. Some newly speaking infants choose to produce words in only certain contexts or in the presence of a chosen few. You may long to show off your child's amazing new skill, but can be disappointed to find that however enthusiastic your approach, no matter how much cajoling you do or how numerous your prompts, your baby will simply refuse to talk for others or repeat a word he could clearly produce the day before. This is not a sign of stubbornness; several influences may be involved in his decision to keep his new words to himself.

At this stage, your baby will probably attribute to a word not only its direct meaning, but a range of meanings that cover a whole context. So, for instance, the word "car" might not, for him, be the appropriate response to your pointing to a vehicle parked in the street because at this time he is using "car" to refer to all his favorite toys at home or simply anything with wheels. Alternatively, you may find that he produces one word to refer to loads of different and seemingly incongruous objects or situations, and this may be simply because it is the word your child finds easiest to say.

Early words remain context-bound for a long time, and it is up to you to expand their meanings and fill in where additional words are missing. So, for example, when your 18-month-old child points to his father who is putting on his coat to leave the house, the word "daddy" may signify not only the person but also the action and the circumstances, that is, "Daddy is putting on his coat to leave the house." By using the only word he has available in his spoken repertoire, your baby is drawing your attention to a much wider meaning and

YOUR CHILD'S VOCABULARY

It is never too early to introduce your baby to the pleasure of books and reading. Just because your baby is not yet able to understand or follow the words, rhymes, or stories you recite, does not mean he isn't enjoying and learning from them. The benefits of reading books are far reaching, from the sounds of the language they contain—its rhythms, grammar, and meanings—to the feel of the book itself and the illustrations therein; all provide fantastic stimulation for the budding language learner. They also stimulate an early love of reading.

From around one year onward, introduce more structured language learning activities into your baby's daily routine. At this age, he will be focused enough to sustain looking at picture books in a detailed way. Play naming games with the images on the page, prompt him to try to repeat new words, and use your imagination to add to the stories or illustrations to make them even more enticing and fun. At first, you may find that you have to perform both sides of such "games"—asking your baby to name the object in a picture, then providing the name yourself. Though your child may not join in much at first, he is processing the information carefully and will eventually take his turn.

Patience is vital with first words. Early speech can be erratic and difficult to understand. This is not the time to start adjusting your child's speech or insisting on correct pronunciation. Nor should you attempt to restrict meaning to single objects. Whenever possible, if your child is proving hard to understand, try to use other cues—body language, tone of voice, gestures—to interpret his vocalizations so that he can see that his attempts at communication are successful and he will be encouraged to keep "talking" to you.

is compensating for the limits of his word-production abilities. At this stage, he has yet to learn that there are words to refer to every action, object, person, or situation. Your baby relies on the positive feedback that his attempts to talk generate, knowing that you, at least, will probably understand his intentions.

First words aren't just about sharing information or communicating needs and desires. By prompting others to respond, they perform another vital role. When your baby says one word to refer to an entire situation, he naturally engages his listener in an exchange. As a result, you or another party talks back, thus providing him with the words he either doesn't possess or can't yet produce himself, thereby not only further strengthening his burgeoning vocabulary but also enhancing his understanding of the rules of spoken interaction. Remember too that once his vocabulary is under way, your baby will soon start to produce as many as 50 new words a week—a budding little linguist.

A name for everything

Initially, word production progresses slowly, and your toddler may utter, at most, a few new words a month. These first words often include phonetic simplifications, whereby your baby might reduce a cluster of difficult consonants into a single, more manageable sound, rendering "smile," for instance, into "mile", "tractor" into "tattor," or "lamb" into "am". This is why it can be difficult for you to distinguish early words from babbles.

Another common simplification is the use of the same consonant throughout a single word, so your baby changes "doggie" into "doddie" or "goggie." In changing the consonant from "d" to "g," your baby will use different muscles and tongue positions in the mouth, so it is much easier for him to repeat the same sound than alternate between them. Keep in mind that in order to make a sound, your baby also has to use his breath and voice at the same time, so it isn't surprising that early words can come out sounding somewhat mixed up. Controlling the vocal apparatus takes a lot of practice—much of which happens when your baby is amusing himself in his crib, "chatting" away to his teddies or mumbling to himself in the stroller.

It can take weeks for a new word to be perfected and spoken correctly, even if it is a common word used in your baby's daily routines and which, to us, is both easy to understand and produce.

The naming explosion

Sometime between eighteen and thirty months of age, a noticeable shift from your baby producing just a handful of recognizable words to suddenly wanting to name everything and everyone in his environment will occur. This is known as "the naming explosion." Researchers believe that several fundamental cognitive developments are responsible for this change; in other words, improvements occur in the way in which your child makes sense of his world.

Decontexualization of words

Before your baby can begin to produce new words at a rapid rate, he must learn to decontextualize words—he has to grasp the idea that words are symbols referring to specific entities in the world instead of names he can use to refer to entire situations, categories, or experiences. This is not as obvious as it may appear. When you hold up a red rubber ball and say "ball," how should your baby know that the single syllable you just uttered only refers to the object in your hand? Couldn't he just as well interpret your utterance as meaning: "I am holding a round object in my left hand?" or believe it to correspond to a particular characteristic of the ball—round or red—instead of the object itself? You probably take it for granted that your child will make the correct link between the spoken word and its specific meaning, but this is not as simple as it may at first appear. Luckily, your baby will be helped by hearing the word "ball" used to refer to similar objects in many different contexts. Also, once he has learned the other words relating to the situation—"hand," "hold," "round," "bouncy"—he can correctly attribute the right meaning to the word you are trying to teach him.

Word acquisition goes farther still. Your baby not only has to realize that each thing has a name, but he also has to discover that a word can apply to a whole category of similar objects, and that some words even have more than one meaning. So "drink," for instance, not only

Research and brain-imaging techniques have shown that areas in both brain hemispheres contribute to language acquisition and processing. As your child matures, however, regions of the left hemisphere will tend to become more specialized for the task. Early on, both hemispheres compete to process all aspects of language but, with development, hemispheric specialization progressively takes place. The right hemisphere tends gradually to predominate in the processing of the more social aspects of language—narratives, jokes, familiar everyday phrases, and certain aspects of intonation that convey subtler meanings. The left hemisphere tends progressively to predominate in processing grammar.

We know this because adults who have damage to the right hemisphere of their brains sometimes speak in a flat or robotic way, with little intonation. They also tend to interpret statements too literally, without understanding or picking up on some of the subtleties of language use. By contrast, those with left-hemisphere damage tend to be able to produce a string of words but in ungrammatical ways.

Brain damage can also provide clues about normal brain function. During the early years of life, when the human brain remains more "plastic," or resilient, than in later years, it is able to adapt to damage in one area by compensating in another. So infants who undergo a brain hemispherectomy (the removal of one hemisphere due, for instance, to epilepsy) are still able to learn language almost faultlessly as the remaining hemisphere takes over all the necessary processing. However, adults who have a hemispheric injury after language has become consolidated, find language relearning more difficult.

Although there is still a lot to learn about how the human brain works, what is clear is that very complex pathways are involved in the process of learning to understand and to produce language—a process that begins in the womb and continues throughout your little one's childhood and even into adolescence.

refers to his favorite juice, but to milk and water, too, as well as to the action of drinking and swallowing. This understanding is linked to the development of object categorization. So "dog" will no longer refer just to his own dog, but to the whole class of dogs. Moreover, once your child is able to partition situations or groups of objects into their elements, it will become easier for him to learn the names for all the different parts involved (for example, the tail, body, and legs of a dog).

Your child's expanding memory and understanding of the rules governing his social and physical environments are also probably involved in the onset of the naming explosion. Studies have also shown that as infants learn new words, they are particularly sensitive to the other cues adults use to communicate their intent. So, in the situation above, your baby will not only pay attention to the word "ball," but also to the direction of your gaze, the tone of your voice—are you happy or sad?—whether you are making a statement or asking a question, as well as other even more subtle clues, such as those apparent from body language and gesturing.

Cracking the language code

Learning a language begins with the task of segmenting it into its distinct parts: from phonemes to single words, to clauses, followed by phrases, and, finally, to sentences. The first problem for your baby is to segment the speech stream. When you talk, you don't leave spaces between words as you do in writing—sounds run into one another. However, babies are amazing in the ways in which they crack the language code.

One study taught children to recognize the sound of a single word, in this case "doctor," by repeating the word many times over. Then the researchers inserted the word into a short passage, such as: "The doctor was a nice man. Mommy liked the doctor and so she visited the doctor often." Babies as young as four months turned their heads more frequently toward passages with the word "doctor" in them than to passages with other words. So, your young baby can segment words out of the continuous speech stream early in his development.

Other research has shown that by the age of six months, your baby will already pay attention to the presence of clauses (groups of words that go together) in speech.

Even before he understands the language he hears, your baby is already aware that sentences are made up of different parts.

For example, it has been shown that your young baby is capable of discriminating correct clause boundaries from incorrect ones. So, even before understanding the meaning, when your six-month-old hears a sentence recited with pauses in the wrong places—such as "the boy who … walked along the … road is tired"—he will show a different response to hearing

the sentence with the correct clause grouping, "the boy … who walked along the road … is tired."

By nine months of age, your infant's sensitivity to language structure will have been refined even more. This coincides with the age at which his own babbling will take on rhythms resembling phrases, with characteristics such as rising intonation and pauses, which segment his stream of babbles.

By around eleven months, at which point language comprehension will be already well under way, he will attend to the meanings of some of the individual nouns and verbs that make up sentences.

Finally, considerably later in development, your baby will pay attention to articles, such as "the" and "a," and to what linguists call "morphemes" (parts of words that carry meaning, such as the suffixes -er and -ed, which indicate the different meanings between, for example, "dance" and "dancer" or "dance" and "danced").

Bilingual babies

As discussed, the task of learning one language, never mind two or three, involves breaking the flow of speech into smaller units that can be organized, made sense of, and remembered. Spoken language contains highly complex, overlapping information. For the learner, it is a little like cracking a code. If yours is a bilingual household, the language challenge is even greater. Luckily for your baby, as we saw in earlier sections, he is equipped with the skills designed to make the job easier for him, skills that you, as an adult, no longer possess.

You probably take talking for granted. However, if you stop to consider what is actually taking place when you speak or listen to others, you will quickly realize just how many things are going on simultaneously. At the most basic level, in all languages, there is no hard-and-fast rule telling the listener where one word ends and the next one begins. You use subtle cues of intonation, stress patterns, and regularities to help yourself distinguish word boundaries. These clues are not immediately obvious to your infant, who is learning language afresh. Furthermore, cues to decode language are not universal: each family of languages is characterized by its own linguistic rhythm. In English, for instance, stress is the most apparent and obvious cue for segmenting speech. We say, "giráffe" not "gíraffe," and we know that the noun "cóntrast" has a different meaning from the verb, "to contrást" In French, howoever, syllable units, as opposed to stress, are the main cues to segmentation. In this language, stress is placed evenly across every syllable in a word. So a baby learning French will not be able to use stress as a reliable rhythmic cue to help him segment the speech stream.

Parents with different backgrounds often worry that speaking to their baby in more than one language might slow language development, considering that the bilingual infant faces the task of learning more than one set of linguistic rules. Some scientists argue that learning more than one language at once in infancy may place obstacles in the way of smooth language acquisition, but others believe that, because of the ease with which babies can learn more than one language, bilingualism may be an advantage. Before his brain becomes specialized, your baby retains the unique ability to distinguish a whole range of sounds from the world's diverse languages. Later on, once he becomes familiar with the language(s) most relevant to his daily life, he will lose this ability. This is why the younger your child is exposed to a language, the easier it will be for him to pick it up.

Helping your child learn two languages

So, far from shielding your young child from multilingual experiences, you should take every opportunity to expose him to different languages. Your bilingual child may have double the number of words to learn and memorize, but this will not slow down his language development and he will more naturally produce the right accent and rhythm for each tongue if his exposure to them is consistent and happens early in life. A good tip, therefore, and one that all bilingual households should try to adhere to, is to have each parent consistently speak to your baby in his or her native language. In this way, your infant grows up with two reliable models—one for each of the languages he is learning. Most toddlers quickly learn to associate one language with one parent and the other language with the other parent. However, if one parent speaks the language of the surrounding environment, then, with time, that language may become the stronger of the two, particularly in terms of speaking. The child will understand both languages fluently, but may start to respond in just one of them, particularly if he has a lot of contact with the outside world.

SINGLE WORDS TO SENTENCES

Once your child has learned 100–150 words, he will begin putting them together to create short phrases. This may occur any time from 18 to 30 months of age. Initially, theses phrases are often made up of two or three words—"daddy ball," or "all gone mommy car." Less important words, such as "the," "but," and "and," are omitted in favor of the words that carry most meaning. The transition from one-word to two- or more-word utterances may seem unremarkable—the meaning still requires a lot of guesswork from the listener—but actually this step shows that your baby has understood some of the complex aspects of language. Although baby talk might sound unsophisticated to your adult ear, if you listen closely, you will find that it often follows simple grammatical rules and can convey somewhat complex meanings.

With the onset of combining words, whole situations are no longer referred to with just a single word. Your toddler will now select from his vocabulary two or three terms that he feels will best encompass the meaning he wants to convey. However, it doesn't stop there—he also has to decide the order in which to put these words. By listening closely to your little one's early phrases, you can follow his progress as he experiments with word order and other rules of grammar and intonation.

Using "pivot" words

At the single-word level, an expression such as "all gone" might be used to express the fact that the child has eaten all his food. However, later, he begins to combine "all gone" with other words in his existing vocabulary to express a variety of meanings. So "all gone daddy" might mean that dad has gone out; "all gone bath" that bath time is finished, and "all gone spoon" that baby has hurled his cutlery on the floor and lunch is well and truly over. Expressions such as "all gone," or other common ones, such as "more" or "mine," are called "pivot" words, and they play an important role in getting grammar off the ground.

Learning plurals

One of the earliest conventions that English-speaking toddlers pick up is the addition of "s" to mark the plural. This may seem an easy step to us, but consider the word "goose," for instance. Why should it not become "gooses" in the plural? And why "two feet" not "two foots"? The English language is full of relatively arbitrary exceptions to its rules, which make the task of learning to speak that much trickier for the child. The early years are full of magical experiences for you, special moments that you never forget. Children's errors are often logical and intelligent, but also completely charming. Even when learning the plural "feet," children may add an "s" and say "feets." An even more interesting example comes from a little girl who enchanted her parents by making the following pluralizing mistake: Katie was two and a half when she learned the song "Head, shoulders, knees and toes, knees and toes ..." For months she delighted everyone with the song. However, some time after her third birthday, her mother noticed something odd in the child's lyrics: Katie was now singing the end of the song with a noticeable mistake, "... and eyes and ears and mouth and no ... head, shoulders, knees and toes, knees and toes." Katie's mom pointed to the little girl's nose and said, "What's that?" Katie answered, "It's my no." Puzzled, Katie's mom asked, "Isn't that your nose?" "No," Katie answered, "I have only one!"

Playing word games

Toddlers like to play word games. You will often hear your little one mumbling to himself or to his toys, re-creating dialogues he has heard or taken part in, or inventing new terms. He may also change the order of the words to convey different meanings. So, for example, your child may say, "sock mommy" when he wants you to put his sock on for him, but "mommy sock" to call your attention to the dog chewing your slipper under the kitchen table. Although these "phrases"are incomplete, they still adhere to basic grammatical rules by using word order and stress to communicate different meanings.

Other noticeable steps in this experimental phase of language development include the appearance of terms that indicate ownership—"my" and "mine"—and the introduction of the past-tense marker "-ed." These are exciting discoveries for your young speaker. Using self-referential terms allows your toddler to assert himself and protect his belongings, while the past tense will open up new avenues of communication. Your child can now clearly refer to events that have already happened. His language is no longer restricted to the here and now, which has, up to that point, been the main focus of his interactions. This also leaves him open to making new mistakes, especially if he is an English-speaking youngster. He will have to get to grips with the fact that verbs sometimes behave in strange ways. For instance, why does "he goes" turn into "he went"? The toddler who has just discovered the past-tense marker is, therefore, showing intelligence, not confusion, when he turns and says, "We goed there, mommy!" instead of "We went there!" In fact, you may find that your young speaker who has been using a word correctly for some time suddenly begins to make surprising

mistakes as new grammatical rules are introduced in his repertoire. Double plurals or tense markers are common errors, so you might hear your little one say "sheeps" or "wented." Yet these so-called "errors" bear witness to how logical and creative your child is.

This is very much a time for diary keeping: the anecdotes you can collect during the early years of speaking make for some of the most priceless moments of parenting.

Little chatterboxes

From the moment your child begins to use recognizable words to communicate, he will test out his vocabulary on you and other adults, and on his peers, too. However, the transition from child–adult to child–child interaction is not as straightforward as it might seem. Interactive exchanges between parents and their baby are usually initiated, guided, and bolstered by the adults, who not only have the ability to take the lead but guarantee some level of mutual comprehension. You will probably be really good at interpreting your toddler's body language, gestures, facial expressions, and utterances, and this understanding will provide a scaffold upon which reciprocal communication can be built. As your child gets better at taking his conversational turn, you will up the ante and encourage more dialogue from him, until he achieves his desired goal—to get a specific message across in words. Talking to a grown-up ends up being satisfying for your little language learner, whose self-confidence and motivation will be enhanced at every interaction.

Toddler-to-toddler chat

Talking with peers is a different story altogether. It involves skills that both young speakers are still in the process of perfecting, and requires a lot of patience—something that few toddlers possess. This explains why your 18-to-24-month-old child, who happily chats away to adults or older children, may become mute in front of other toddlers or may even revert to babbling. There is little research into toddler–toddler discourse, but what has been shown is that young talkers have great difficulty establishing what knowledge they can take for granted and what needs to be spelled out when addressing peers. When faced with another novice talker, a toddler who wants to inform his friend that his brother stole his ball might announce, "Jimmy took it!" without explaining who Jimmy is, or what he took. Young children find it difficult to assess other people's knowledge or level of comprehension in any given situation. They assume too much and say too little. This inevitably leads to confusion on both sides. Because both the spoken message and the feedback it receives are incongruous, like parallel play in which toddlers play alongside each other instead of with each other, what often happens in dialogue between young speakers is that they end up having "conversations" in parallel about things that may or may not be related. This is why early child–child conversations tend to be egocentric and are more like parallel monologues than interactive dialogues. Each toddler talks about his own experience. If there does happen to be a conversational overlap,

it is probably due more to the shared context than to the actual content of the verbal exchange. The "conversation" didn't even have a mutual topic, but both toddlers will probably choose to talk about something in the immediate context. As a result, toddlers tend to seek shared situations instead of shared knowledge so that they can establish and maintain some degree of shared verbal understanding with their peers.

Although we still have a lot to learn about how young speakers acquire language, it is clear that toddler–toddler discourse presents a special challenge to your developing child. It fails to provide him with many of the scaffolding cues, prompts, and support mechanisms available in toddler–parent exchanges. So much so that it has been found that babies who spend more time communicating with peers than with adults—because they spend their days at nursery, for instance—acquire language somewhat more slowly. However, this is not detrimental to overall language development. There is also evidence that for some children, the busy environment of day care actually encourages language production.

Twins and language

Twins are interesting because they often develop a special "twin language" of their own, characterized by serious mispronunciations that render their speech unintelligible to others. They babble away, seeming to understand one another, while others around them scratch their heads and frown. This twin-tongue is probably more about nonverbal cues than anything else; the siblings are so well attuned to one another that they don't need words to communicate. This is probably why twins are commonly slower in acquiring language than other children. They spend so much time interacting together that they miss out on some of the language support that parents can supply. That said, the delay is negligible and does not affect the way twins speak later in life. All in all, unless your child has an actual speech impediment or language delay, whether he begins talking at one or at two and a half, he will, at some point, end up as a little chatterbox.

4

How your baby learns to move

YOUR BABY'S MOTOR DEVELOPMENT

During your baby's first 24 months of life, she will nearly quadruple in weight and double in height. Her head, which is already large in comparison to the rest of her body at birth, will continue to grow, increasing in circumference by almost one-third. These developments make the job of learning to move one of the hardest tasks your baby will face in her early months. As she explores her environment, she not only has to adapt to each new experience she encounters, but she must also continually adjust her behavior to the demands of her changing body.

Scientists used to think of motor development in terms of stages and milestones, focusing on factors, such as body size, muscle mass, improved coordination, and brain maturity, to explain improvements in motor abilities. However, recent research has shown us that instead of developing along smooth and predictable curves, infant growth is characterized by fits and starts, and a child's mastery of motor skills is often a case of two steps forward, one step back.

Psychologists studying child development now believe that motor development is more about learning to learn, with babies becoming more agile as a result of their improved capacities for learning, instead of straightforward factors, such as increased muscle strength or better motor coordination.

Different motor skills

Motor development involves gross motor skills, such as rolling over, sitting, crawling, and walking, and fine motor skills, such as manual dexterity. Together, over time, the two skill types gradually transform a newborn infant from a reflex-driven, helpless being into an independent toddler.

Although growth curves and weight charts are used to monitor a child's progress, it is important to remember that development doesn't occur in clear-cut stages. Every little step in your baby's progress is dependent upon a host of interrelated factors, from physical changes to improvements in brain function, from her experiences, temperament, and cultural background to the social feedback she receives at every stage. All these facets of development are intricately bound together. This is why different children reach milestones at different ages and develop along their own unique trajectories. Indeed, some babies sit and crawl early but don't walk for a frustratingly long time, while others may miss out the crawling phase altogether and progress straight from sitting to walking.

Learning to control movement

The body is a complicated machine that requires a vast amount of experience and practice in order to learn to control its movements. Everyday actions, such as walking to a chair, sitting down, reaching for a light switch, or turning over a page seem simple to adults; we perform them all the time without thinking. To the growing child, however, they present endless challenges. In this chapter, you will discover just how amazing tiny feats of development, such as picking up a spoon or taking a single step, really are. In fact, every purposeful action your baby makes is a triumph in its own right. For instance, in the act of reaching for a soft toy that you hold out for her, your child has to gauge both the size of the object and how far away it is from her, select the right posture, and work out how to maintain her balance while at the same time reaching forward for it, not with one hand but with both hands, opening them to the right degree to grasp the toy. In doing this, she has to coordinate the movements of her arms with the information provided by her visual system and her muscles must allow for the movement of her trunk as she reaches, then compensate for the weight of the toy that she must grasp in a certain way, depending on what it's made of.

Breaking down the complexities of such purpose-driven movements as these can help parents to better understand the challenges their children face as they learn to use their bodies. So next time your young child performs a new trick, however small, remind yourself of all the effort that went into it—clapping hands or climbing up a single step will never look the same to you again.

Early movements

At birth, your baby becomes subject to the forces of gravity. Inside the womb, the amniotic liquid provided buoyancy so that her head and limbs were easy to support and move around, but now that she is outside, they feel like lead weights to her tiny newborn muscles. At this early stage, your infant's movements are largely reflex driven (see also Chapter 1), and her first few weeks of life are spent in the fetal position (see the box, opposite).

Although this curled-up posture may seem restrictive, a newborn is already able to move from A to B, albeit involuntarily. The strong grasping reflex that prompts your baby to tighten her fingers around anything that comes into contact with her palms, coupled with the alternating movements of the kicking reflex, can propel her along certain surfaces. This explains why instead of being at the lower end of her crib—where you put her for her nap—you may occasionally find your newborn either curled up near the top of her bed or lying across the mattress. Unknowingly, her tiny hands have probably grasped the sheet, which has

MORE ABOUT **THE STEPPING REFLEX**

During the first few weeks after birth, if you hold your newborn upright with her feet just touching a solid surface, she will automatically begin flexing and extending her legs in an alternating walking action. Scientists are still unsure exactly why this happens. Clearly the drive to walk is a particularly strong one in human development, but what is not clear is why it should appear so early on, when the legs cannot support the body and coordination is not yet established. This reflex is only visible for the first six to eight weeks, after which weight gain outstrips muscle strength and your infant is only able to manage flexing and extending her legs when she is lying down. In this position, gravity assists the hip joints to support the legs. Some researchers have argued that the stepping reflex never actually disappears during infant development; it just subsides into leg kicking in the supine position.

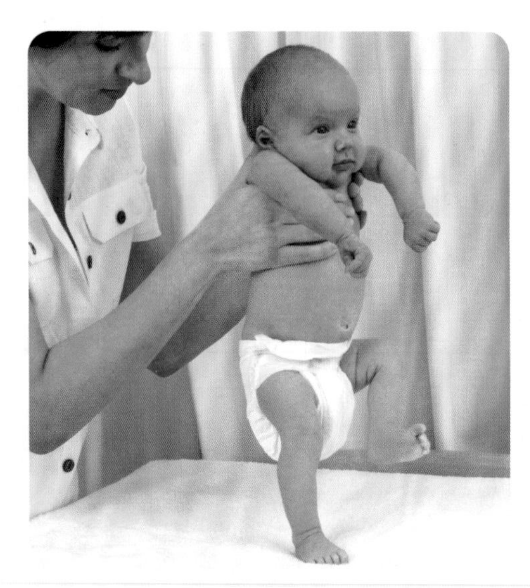

THE FETAL POSITION

Newborns tend to lie all curled up—behavior left over from their time in the womb—due to their lack of muscular strength and control over their limbs. If you place your baby on his belly, his arms and legs will be bent inward under his body. If you place him on his back (recommended for sleeping), his arms and legs will be bent in the air and drawn toward his body.

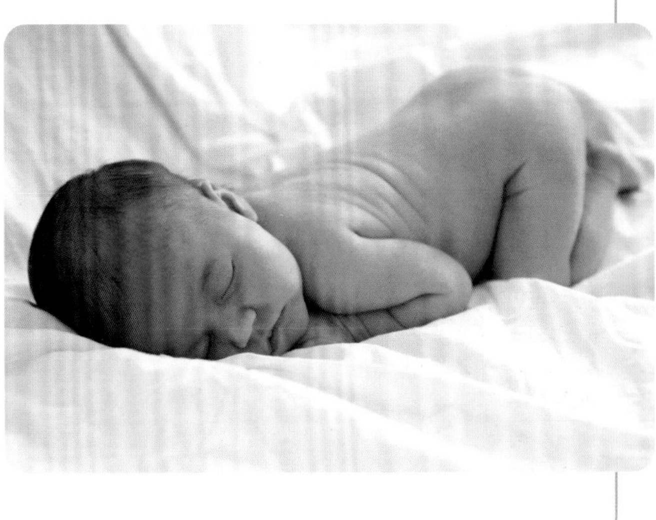

changed her position. Such creeping is slow and gradual, and it generally occurs during sleep. It has been suggested that babies do this to bring the tops of their heads in contact with a solid surface—perhaps re-creating the sensation of being cocooned by the walls of the womb. It may also act as a useful means of preventing overheating, because it enables your infant to work herself free of covers when she is feeling too warm. This is why you are advised to always place your baby on her back so that her feet touch the lower end of her crib. It is also recommended that you cover her with several thin blankets that can easily be discarded (instead of one heavy quilt).

Newborns extend their limbs fully only when they actively kick or flay their arms, which is generally in response to internal stimuli, such as discomfort or the impulse to stretch or yawn, or as a result of external stimuli, such as the sound of your voice, a caress, or a sudden noise that causes a start (see page 15).

One of the most noticeable features of early motor behavior, and one that is directly affected by the pull of gravity, is the newborn stepping reflex (see the box, opposite).

A gradual process

Learning to control the body is all about learning to adjust to change. A movement performed to achieve a specific outcome, such as raising a hand to one's face, requires different actions at different stages of development, because the proportions of the body parts involved alter and the strength of the muscles change. There may also be clothing to take into account, restrictions due to posture, and a range of specific intentions behind the action. A seven-week-old fetus will need to raise her short arm buds at the shoulder to touch her face, whereas a seven-week-old infant will have to deeply bend her arm at both the elbow and the shoulder and control the position of her hand. Similarly, a seven-month-old baby who has become an expert at controlling both posture and head position to look straight ahead, when sitting will suddenly have to find new postural strategies to achieve the same goal when she begins to crawl on all fours, and later hoists herself to cruise along furniture.

Supporting her head

Many species of mammals are able to support their heads at birth. Some even get to their feet and walk within minutes of emerging from the womb. Human babies, by contrast, are born with little control over their mobility. Evolution has given humans large brains in proportion to their bodies, which is why your newborn can barely support her heavy head and children look top-heavy throughout the first years of life. Neck control, therefore, is one of the earliest developmental milestones of motor coordination. It is a gradual process that is quickly noticeable but not actually totally perfected until the latter half of the first year, when your child is finally able to control and alter her head posture in response to a multitude of subtle auditory and visual cues.

At birth

Your newborn's neck muscles are so weak and her head so heavy that she is only able to hold it upright for a matter of seconds and turn it from side to side when lying down or supported in your arms. This is why she always needs some head support, whether she is sitting in a car seat or being carried or cradled. At this stage, the head movements she makes—when turning toward a sound, for instance, or to root toward a nipple for a feed—are the result of involuntary reflexes and are brief and unsteady. Yet, at each new attempt, your baby makes a tiny improvement in neck control. Parents pay little attention to these minor triumphs of motor development, but behind every twitch, every head lift, or turn your baby performs, there are clusters of muscles at work, reacting in complex ways to changes both from inside your baby's body and from the environment.

By measuring tiny changes in muscle activity and tension, scientists have been able to ascertain how the immature body progressively responds to gravity and becomes fine-tuned for the task of controlled action.

Support will be required *for your baby's head and neck until her muscles are strong enough for her to raise her head on her own. To encourage her to raise her head, try placing a rolled-up towel under her chest when she's awake and lying on her front.*

Four to six weeks of age

Your little one will have gained enough strength and coordination to lift and turn her head when lying down on her front, or to hold it erect for a short while when supported upright. She still needs a cupped hand at the ready for support at all times, however, because her head control is still somewhat precarious. However, her new ability means that she can now start to actively choose what she looks at, as well as to change the angle at which she observes things close up. These brief moments of head control fuel her desire to improve her coordination. She can now start to track moving objects and try to locate interesting sounds in her environment. The world is becoming more exciting for your little one.

Babies who are frequently placed on their stomachs when they are awake often achieve head-and-neck control a little earlier than those who spend most of their waking time lying on their backs. Of course, young babies should be placed on their stomachs only when awake and supervised.

Research has clearly shown that sleeping in the prone position increases the chances of sudden infant death syndrome (SIDS).

Babies should always be put to sleep on their backs at the lower half of the crib. However, there are little games you can play to help your baby improve head control (see below):

- After a diaper change, or at other times when your infant is alert and on a safe surface, try rolling her over onto her stomach and encouraging her to lift up and turn her head to look around or to turn toward your voice.
- Lying her on her stomach across your lap is another good position from which your little one can practice lifting her head.

By four months

If you place your baby on her front , she should now be able to lift her head to 45 degrees and look around, and when seated in a chair or held in your arms, she will quickly learn to maintain and alter her head posture. However, it will be another several months before your little one will be coordinated enough to hold her head steady in response to motion, such as in a moving car or a stroller. Once head control is under way, your baby is able to focus her attention on hand–eye coordination, which opens up a whole world of new possibilities.

Swiping

Right from birth, your infant will move her arms and legs. Initially, these are not directed at anything but are involuntary reflex actions occurring in response to physical stimulation. Although they serve no intentional purpose, they help to increase muscle strength and coordination. Within a few weeks, however, your little one will have gained enough control over her limbs to begin to stretch her arms out intentionally in the direction of objects that have captivated her attention. At this stage, she is not yet reaching to grasp and take hold of objects; she is merely swiping at them. Her movements are still crude and she cannot yet control her hands or fingers. However, fascinatingly, research has shown that infants tend to only swipe at objects that are roughly within reach, suggesting that long before they are able to reach properly, their brains have already processed vital information about distance and some of the rules governing spatial relationships.

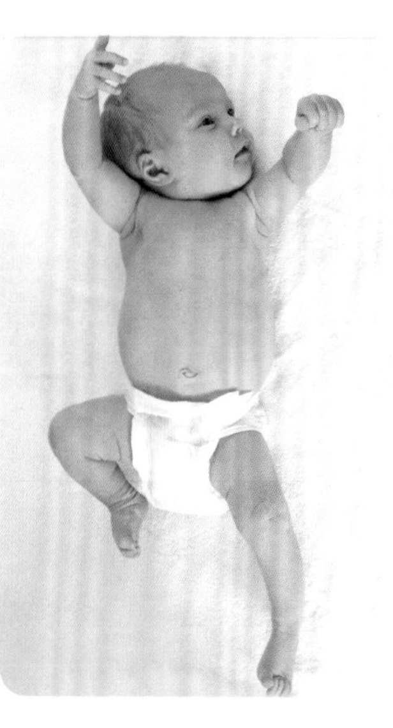

Crude movements of the arms toward objects are one of the earliest visible manifestations of goal-oriented behavior in young infants.

You are no doubt aware that moving her arms toward an object requires a lot of effort on your baby's part; she seems to strain every single muscle in her body just to be able to move her wayward arm. Moreover, every action, however crude, is embedded in other actions; lifting an arm toward an object involves coordinating visual information with limb control, then moving the arm from the shoulder while at the same time keeping it straight and maintaining overall balance.

Motor development broadly progresses from the top down, and from the center out to the extremities. Your baby will master head control before she can maintain an upright posture, she will sit before she stands, and she will learn to move her arms before she masters the finer motor control involved in grasping. The pathways in the brain responsible for perceiving and locating things in the environment develop earlier than the networks responsible for producing voluntary action. So, while your young infant is adept at locating a sound or light, for instance, she has difficulty controlling her actions sufficiently to smoothly track a moving noise or light with her eyes and head.

Fascinating new studies suggest that babies may be born with a propensity for visual-manual exploration. It has been found that if placed in a room with the lights dimmed, newborns will move their arms toward a beam of light to bring their hands into view. So although they are still too young to make proper use of their limbs, they strive to keep both hands in sight. This is amazing, considering at this stage they probably don't even realize that these hands belong to them. It has also been found that long before they can reach or grab hold of objects, especially young infants already orient themselves toward interesting objects with both their eyes and the direction their arms point toward. The swipe that may then ensue will be crude—a wobbly wave in the general direction of the coveted object and, if the baby is lucky, her clenched fist may actually make brief contact with the object.

These attempts are not meaningless. Every new effort strengthens connections in the brain and reinforces your baby's desire to try again. At a few weeks of age, your baby's fingers start to uncurl and she is able to begin swiping at objects with open hands. This further increases her chances of contact with targets and even the occasional momentary grasp, leading her to discover just how useful her little hands are for exploring the world.

HOW *you can help*

ENCOURAGING SWIPING

Every time your baby uses her muscles performing a movement that involves coordination, she gets closer to gaining control over her body. Swiping is good practice for later reaching and grasping, and you can actively encourage it during her first couple of months of life. Hang an interesting mobile just above the changing table, low enough for your baby's arm to reach up and just touch it. When she is lying underneath it, calm and alert, attract her attention to an object on the mobile and make it gently move across her field of vision. She will probably fixate on it for a while as she works out what she wants to do. Then she will extend her arm excitedly upward.

If she does not make contact, move the mobile down slightly so that it touches her hand, thereby showing her that her actions can produce some interesting results.

If she does not make any effort to swipe from this position, try picking her up toward the mobile, or use an interesting toy, such as a rattle, and shake it a few inches away from her. Keep in mind that posture and gravity play significant roles in complicating or facilitating motor control at this early age. Moving the arms while reclining in a baby chair or bouncer will require a different amount of strength than doing so in the supine position. Babies as young as three weeks make attempts to swipe at objects, so why not make it a daily workout? It can be a lot of fun for both of you, and it may give you a chance to witness the first of many little triumphs that will mark your baby's exciting journey through motor development.

Holding and exploring

For the first few weeks of life, your baby's fingers will grip onto anything that comes into contact with her palms—clothing, fingers, other people's hair, etc. Initially, this kind of grasping is not intentional—although it provides stimulation for her sense of touch—but it creates opportunities for learning, and grasping soon becomes intentional. Two and three month olds will actively try to bring objects that are placed in their hands up to their faces and into their mouths for oral exploration. This is because the nerve endings in the mouth are far more sensitive than those in the hands. So the mouth is an excellent place for early investigations. At this age, however, the behavior is not guided by a set goal. Instead, discoveries occur by chance, out of circumstances; an item finds its way into your baby's grip, a series of crude movements partially driven by reflexes position the object within your baby's field of vision or in her mouth, and exploration ensues. The drive to bring the hands up to the face, particularly the mouth region for

MORE ABOUT **HOW COORDINATION DEVELOPS**

Becoming a coordinated individual doesn't simply involve learning how to move the head, trunk, arms, legs, hands, and feet; it also involves gaining control over the eyes.

The information provided by the visual system plays a central role in maintaining balance and posture, and is obviously crucial for planning and completing purposeful actions. Being able to locate, focus on, and track a moving object is one of the primary hurdles faced by your newborn's immature visual system.

Your baby actually possesses the ability to move her eyes at birth, but like arm coordination, the early movements of her eyes lack accuracy. She can follow an object that is close and moves slowly enough for her to focus on, but to keep on target, she will have to segment the path her eyes take into smaller, more manageable chunks, which are called saccades, whereas when you follow a moving target, your eyes make a single continuous arc.

It takes considerable time, maturity, and practice for eye control to be perfected, but luckily for her, much of your baby's waking time is spent attending to the right visual stimuli.

exploration, seems to develop from life in the uterus, when she had a tendency to bring her fist to her mouth and suck on her fingers or thumbs. In the uterus, however, this was purely reflexive and her mouth simply opened in response to the sensation of her fingers coming into contact with it. This hand-to-mouth behavior continues after birth, becoming increasingly intentional, until by five months of age, your baby anticipates the arrival of her hands and therefore opens her mouth well before her fingers make contact with her lips.

Manipulation skills develop gradually

Before four months of age, your baby will both look at and mouth objects that are placed in her hands, but she does not have the manual dexterity or the hand–eye coordination needed to purposefully finger, mouth or handle them. As she gets older, her manipulation of objects will become increasingly sophisticated, and she will use more and more of her senses to learn about the objects' properties. By the second half of her first year, as she increasingly masters the new skill of reaching and grabbing—instead of simply holding onto a toy to bring it to her mouth—your little one will pass the toy from one hand to the other; investigate it with her fingertips; chew, suck, pull on, or squash it; and bang it on the floor or on another object to see what sound it makes, thereby discovering with utter delight that the world of objects has endless fun-potential.

Although your baby's sense of touch may have been stimulated before birth, it is only from around four months of age onward that she will begin to actively manipulate objects for the purpose of discovering their properties.

Faces and moving objects are what captures a baby's visual attention most during their first few months and the greatest improvement in visual tracking occurs between six and fourteen weeks of age. So this is a great time for daily "looking" games. Use attention-grabbing objects that either make an interesting noise or are decorated with high-contrast patterns or colors.

Visual tracking

Move a toy slowly back and forth across her field of vision and encourage her to follow it. Keep your movements slow and simple at first, moving the object smoothly across your baby's visual field. If the movement is centered or rotates in one place, this will hold her attention, but it won't exercise her visual system nearly as well as having her practice tracking across her visual field. In time, you can make an object travel faster and begin varying its trajectories.

Once your baby is adept at tracking, try altering the game. Introduce an element of surprise by suddenly changing the direction of the toy or making it stop suddenly. Your baby, having correctly anticipated the end point of the toy's trajectory, may show surprise at the object's unexpected behavior, indicating that she had learned certain rules governing the movement of objects.

Try hiding the toy

Another interesting experiment you can try is to use a screen (such as a book held upright) to hide part of a toy's trajectory. Gradually, your baby will learn to anticipate the object's reappearance and move her eyes to the place where it will reappear before it actually does. (Babies as young as five months can correctly predict where and when a moving object will end up.) And, of course, she will show surprise when a toy moving in a certain direction disappears behind a screen but fails to emerge on the other side to complete the course of its trajectory.

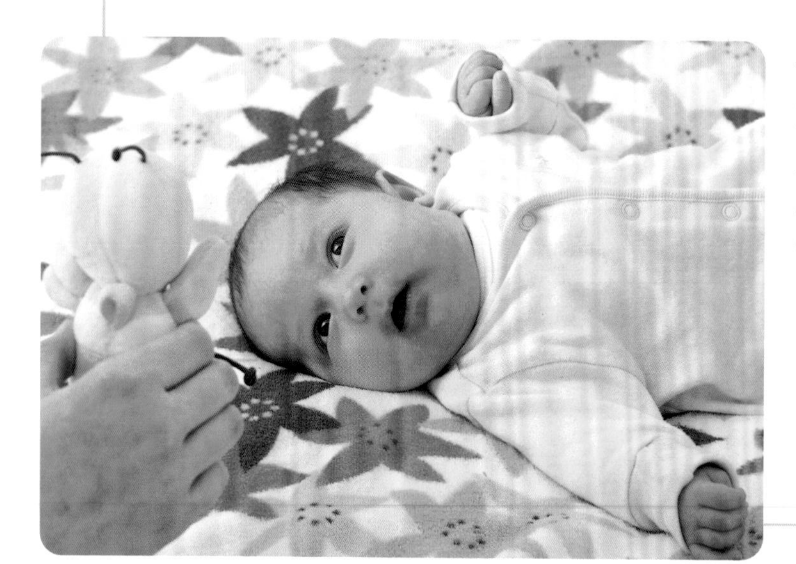

Learning to reach

Once visual tracking and swiping have been mastered, your baby is ready for something more challenging. Reaching occurs as a result of weeks of practice involving a great deal of trial and error. Through her early looking and swiping experiences, your baby has been able to form memories of which movements were successful and which were not. Success motivates her to reproduce the same arm movements in different situations, until she gradually becomes more efficient at reaching for objects that she perceives are within reach. However, her body posture will still place constraints on these efforts. For instance, if she is not yet able to sit unsupported, she will have difficulty reaching with one arm if she is propped up in a sitting position. Generally, in this case, she will opt for a two-handed reach, or use other parts of her body to achieve the desired result.

Research has shown that infants actually start to reach with their feet more than four weeks before they begin reaching with their hands.

Reaching for an object is not as simple as it might at first appear. Your baby's efforts are compounded by many variables, including her posture and center of gravity; her level of muscular strength and coordination; the proportions of her body; the size and shape of the object; its texture, weight, and position relative to her; and even such factors as clothing, which may hinder her arm's flexibility and reach.

Scientists have discovered interesting differences between the way infants and adults reach for things by carefully mapping babies' movements with video data and computer analysis. Similar to swiping and visual tracking, infant reaching is made up of a series of separate movement units, or submovements, instead of of single bell-shape movements.

Stages in reaching

At around four months of age, when your baby begins to reach instead of swipe, a single reaching action toward a desired toy might consist of up to five separate submovements. This is not to say that she makes five separate attempts before getting it right. Instead, she has worked out that moving her arms a little at a time allows her to correct her aim while she is in the process of reaching. This is the best strategy to employ within her limited abilities, because, at such a young age, she still struggles to make her limbs behave exactly as she wants them to, and she still has difficulty predicting the exact outcome of a single, large-scale motor command. There is, however, one interesting exception to this rule. If your baby intends only to hit the target object instead of to grab it, she will take her chances on a single arm movement, probably because it requires far less precision than reaching out to actually grasp a toy.

By the age of about five months your baby will have gained extensive knowledge about spatial relationships and has acquired good eye, arm, and hand coordination. This allows her to accomplish accurate reaching in all kinds of different situations. However, it is important not to confuse reaching with pointing. If your five month old stretches an arm out toward something that is clearly out of reach, it is probable that she is trying to alert your attention to it so that you can get it for her. Interestingly, a baby of this age does not intentionally stretch out to grasp objects that are clearly beyond her reach, demonstrating that she (or her brain) already knows a lot about estimating distances and has realized that such efforts would be pointless.

The ability to reach accurately for stationary objects appears between three and five months. By 18 weeks, your baby is able to start intercepting moving objects. Once again, she approaches this task by breaking it down into movement units—speeding up, slowing down and adjusting the direction of her arm as it moves toward its target. By nine months of age, your baby will have become expert enough at reaching that she stops making a grab for a moving object if she sees an obstruction along its route, and she will be accurate enough to be able to grasp noisy objects in the dark if she perceives them to be within reach. What's more, by this stage, she begins anticipating the size and shape of the object she is reaching for, even if it is concealed from sight. Experiments have shown that nine month olds correctly reach in the dark using both arms if the object they hear nearby sounds large (a deep-sounding gong, for instance), while they will opt for a single-handed, pincer-grip reach if the object sounds small (such as a high-pitched bell). This is quite a feat, considering the level of motor and perceptual coordination involved in processing such information.

Intercepting moving objects

Another amazing skill that your baby will display during the second half of her first year is the ability to intercept moving objects. We've already discussed just how difficult tracking movement with the eyes can be, but add to this the need to maintain posture while simultaneously moving the limbs toward a moving target, and it is easy to imagine the hurdles your little one faces in seemingly simple, everyday actions.

Reaching for a moving object requires careful planning. To grab a ball swinging on the end of string, for example, your baby must anticipate the ball's speed and trajectory to decide how best to intercept it. Initially, this may prove too difficult, and many of her attempts will result in failure. Undeterred, however, she will persist until she finds the best strategy. If the ball is moving from her right to her left, instead of choosing to reach with her right hand (initially the one nearest to the ball), she'll discover the importance of anticipation, and that reaching with her left hand will give her more time to move before the toy disappears out of reach again.

Thus, what seem at first to be simple motor actions turn out to be impressively complex intellectual acts, involving being able to judge distance, speed, and size, and the planning of a series of interrelated actions.

Rolling over

Being able to change positions from lying on her stomach to staring up at the ceiling, or vice versa, is another important motor development. It opens up your baby's visual horizons and gives her the first taste of moving around by herself. It can even serve as an aid to grasping by allowing her to roll to objects that are out of immediate arm's reach.

Your baby will begin rocking from side to side sometime after two months of age. Within a few weeks of mastering this rocking motion, she will discover, often with some surprise, that if she rolls hard enough and twists her body around at the same time, she ends up in a completely new position. It is easier to roll over from the prone position (lying on her stomach) than it is from the supine position (lying on her back), and, therefore, the former tends to occur earlier than the latter.

Rolling over involves strenuous moving, stretching, and planning. Your baby has to shift her center of gravity enough to tip the balance of her weight in the desired direction. She uses her arms and legs as levers, and her head acts a little like a pendulum, its weight helping to create momentum to propel her body. While rolling over from front to back may happen by accident, rolling over from the supine position requires intentionality from the outset. Your baby actively strives to achieve this through much practice. It involves a combination of complicated movements, including arching her body backward, throwing back her head, and twisting one leg around and the other under to finally push her upper trunk over onto her front. It is a real accomplishment that consumes a lot of energy. However, she is rewarded by the knowledge that she has found a new form of mobility. Now, the way she faces when she is lying down is no longer your decision but entirely hers—and, if she can successfully complete the action several times, she can make her way from one end of a rug to the other.

Interestingly, some babies seem to spend weeks happily rocking to and fro without bothering to roll over completely. Others, once they master the skill, choose always to roll in the same direction. Practicing rolling over often happens when unobserved, at bedtime or while you're not paying attention to your baby.

At this age, infants have no concept or fear of depth, and they do not perceive the danger of falling from one surface onto another, so rolling over can lead to accidents. If you are in the habit of taking your baby to bed with you, it is a good idea to place pillows on the floor around the mattress in case she squirms or rolls about at night. Similarly, never turn your back on your baby when she's on the changing table. She could surprise you with a sudden movement that you didn't realize she had mastered and fall off the edge.

Sitting up

Your baby's motor coordination will improve on a regular basis, and new developments may occur simultaneously that may not always be to her advantage. For example, a skill perfected in the supine position, such as reaching or kicking, may become a hindrance in the sitting position; a strategy that may be useful for reaching accurately is not necessarily going to be transferable to other tasks, such as rolling over or sitting up. Human bodies function as complicated machines, with all parts interlinked, so that movement in one area can create disequilibrium in a different area, and tension in one set of muscles will impact on the calibration of other sets of muscles, and so on. In addition, your infant faces the ongoing constraints placed upon her by the immediate environment in which she finds herself.

Baby chairs, rockers, adjustable strollers, and slings may enable your baby to experience the world from an upright or sitting position at an especially young age. However, resting in a supported sitting posture is not the same as sitting up unaided. To maintain a sitting position, your baby must first be able to hold her head erect, have good control over her upper trunk, be able to maintain her center of gravity while creating a steady support base with her legs positioned wide apart. The degree of motor control and strength to achieve this takes several months to develop, which is why sitting up unaided only occurs in the second half of the first year. However, this should not stop you from using baby chairs and the like much earlier—babies love to spend time in different positions, taking in the world from varying angles.

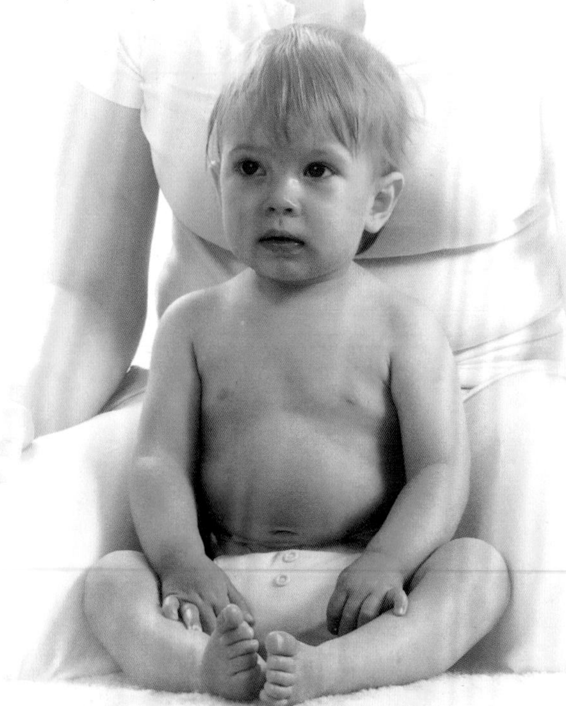

At around two months of age, your infant will have developed enough head control to enjoy spending time in a semisitting position in a suitably supportive baby chair or stroller, as long as it is tipped back far enough to prevent her from tipping forward. While this position affords her a wider view of her environment, she will remain fairly passive sitting in this position; she will make few attempts to move her arms and legs, and will be simply content to contemplate her surroundings from this new angle of vision. By 15 weeks, however, she will need less support and may begin making more efforts to propel herself forward in preparation for the unaided sitting position.

Being able to stay upright without support frees up your baby's hands for manual exploration. This is one of the many reasons that fuel her drive to sit unaided.

At around six months, your little one's muscles will be strong enough to maintain balance unsupported, although only momentarily at first. If placed in a sitting position on the floor, surrounded by pillows, your baby will be able to maintain the posture for a few seconds. However, it will take several weeks of practice before she is both steady and strong enough to lever herself into the position without help, and sit happily for any length of time.

A new view

By eight or nine months, your baby should be a proficient sitter. She will also have learned to coordinate a whole range of other movements, such as turning, reaching, and pointing, while maintaining this posture. One of the most difficult obstacles for a baby learning to sit is finding the correct center of gravity to keep her upper body erect. Establishing and maintaining balance is difficult, with a lot of room for error. Leaning forward or backward or to the side a tiny bit too far can shift her body weight enough to capsize her whole body. This is why your baby will often wobble awkwardly for several seconds when first sitting before finding the right balance.

Babies discover different ways of achieving the correct center of gravity. Some adopt a lotus position, using their legs and feet bent in toward the body to steady their weight slightly forward. Others prefer to sit with their legs wide apart, creating a triangular base. Both positions increase the support base and are good ways to avoid tipping over, because the legs can be used to counterbalance any shifts in body weight.

Helping intellectual development

Sitting up is an important developmental milestone, not only in terms of motor coordination and control, but also in terms of intellectual development. Your baby's visual range when lying down is far more restricted than it is when she is upright. In the sitting position, especially when unrestrained, she can scan a room up and down; turn her head and twist her trunk around to extend her field of vision; bend forward and to the side to alter her focus; and, above all, she can use her hands to reach for and touch all the interesting things around her.

Sometime between six and eight months, your baby will start to reach freely in a sitting position. To achieve this, she must be able to expertly balance her head while maintaining a steady trunk and a leg posture that will provide a reliable base. Babies characteristically adopt a "tripod" position with both legs outstretched in a V shape and one arm leaning on the floor for support. This is a good solution for the novice sitter, but it causes problems for reaching, because the action's goal is now compromised by the need to maintain posture.

If your baby previously was expert at grabbing hold of things, she may suddenly stop reaching with two hands, for instance, or may find her reach restricted by an inability to stretch forward in the new unsupported sitting position. As your baby tries to perfect her reaching, she will stretch her sitting posture to its limits and on occasions may fall forward. Only by eight to ten months of age, and after your baby has been sitting for at least a couple of months, will she understand that she needs to lean her weight forward slightly if she is going to reach with two arms. This is a classic example of how motor development often progresses; skills and strategies are generally not transferable from one motor ability to another, so new solutions must continually be found. Lifting her arms causes a shift in her body's center of mass. In fact, her balance is constantly affected—even taking a breath can alter her center of gravity. In attempting the new task of reaching in the sitting position, your baby faces similar challenges to the adult skier who swaps her skis for a snowboard and has to relearn the skills of getting down the mountain in one piece.

BABY GYMNASTICS

There are many games you can play with your baby to encourage motor coordination. Even from an especially young age, experiencing the world from different positions expands your baby's knowledge of her environment. Objects alter in appearance when viewed from different angles, textures and surfaces can vary depending on how you come into contact with them, and noises can sound different heard from a variety of different places.

To give your infant a wide range of experiences, it's good to hold, carry, or place her in varying positions—across your lap on her stomach, on the floor on her back, lying on one side in her crib, or propped upright against your shoulder. Lifting your baby up into the air above your head will also give her thrilling new sensations of movement and gravity, as well as a glimpse of the world from a high vantage point.

Regular workouts can also be a lot of fun and are excellent opportunities for trying out new movements safely. When she is lying on her back, take your baby's hands and pull her slightly, but let her help to lift her head and neck. This will strengthen her arm and neck muscles and encourages her progressively to take control of the movement herself.

Next, flex her legs and let her press the soles of her feet against the palm of your hand. This will help to exercise her knee and thigh muscles, as well as the pelvic area.

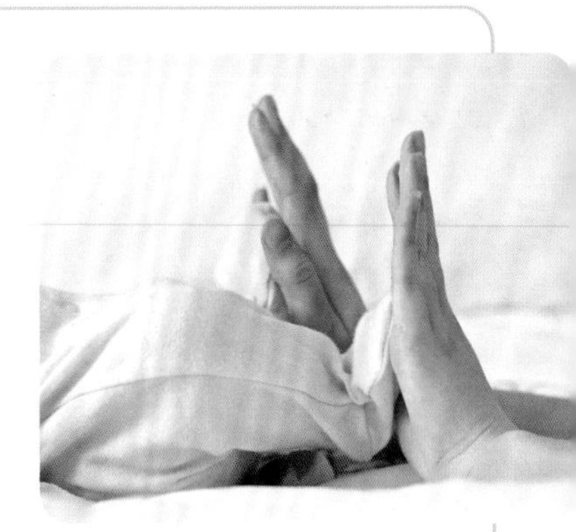

If she is alert, turn her over onto her stomach and then call to her or shake a rattle just above her head to spur her to try to lift and support her head and upper body; this will also help to strengthen her neck and back muscles.

Finally, encourage your baby to recognize her own potential to roll over and sit up by rocking her to and fro and holding her briefly upright before letting her feel the natural pull of her body weight tipping her gently over. Make these activities more enjoyable for your baby by offering enthusiastic encouragement every time she achieves a new position, whether with or without your help.

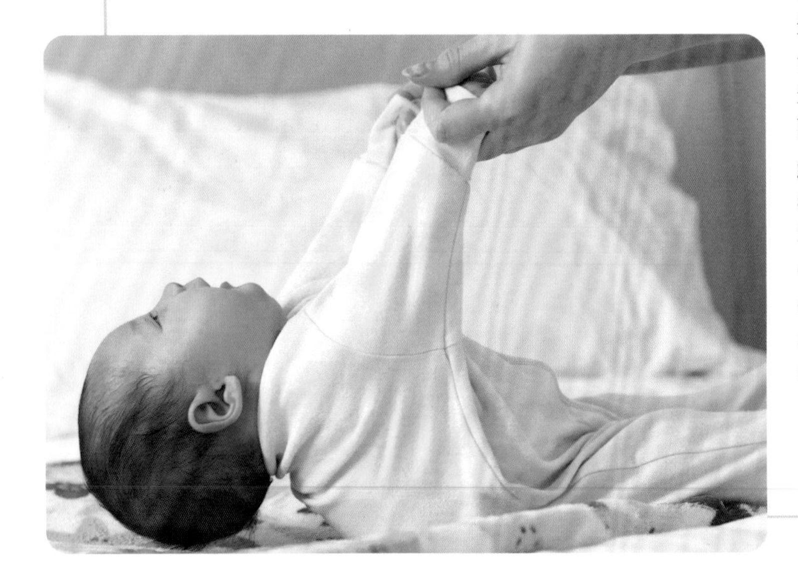

Crawling

Before looking at how your baby progresses from being a stationary sitter to a busy crawler, there is a little task you can do to help gain insight into just what an achievement becoming mobile is. Without getting down on the floor and trying it out, try to describe the series of movements that makes up a crawl. Considering that you have seen many children crawl, and that in the past you've probably done this movement thousands of times yourself, the action sequence should be obvious. However, you'll quickly discover that describing it isn't nearly as straightforward as you thought.

In an amusing experiment, researchers asked this very question of parents, and found that adults were somewhat stumped when put on the spot. They gave all kinds of different descriptions of crawling, the most common being that babies move their left arm and left leg simultaneously, followed by the right arm and right leg. However, maintaining balance with one's body weight shifting completely from side to side at every move is near impossible. Another suggestion was that both arms moved ahead of both legs, but that would result in slow movement. In many cases, adults finally had to resort to getting down on the floor to try it for themselves ... well go on then, give it a try, because it's the only way that you'll be sure.

MORE ABOUT **CRAWLING COORDINATION**

Using transparent surfaces over which infants are made to crawl, scientists have been able to discover the exact pattern of interlimb coordination responsible for hands-and-knees crawling.

Babies who crawl in the regular, all-fours way—as opposed to the more unusual forms of early locomotion, such as bottom scooting—alternate between the two pairs of diagonal limbs to create a "dynamic balance system," like a trotting dog. This is by far the most efficient way of moving forward on all

fours. The center of gravity is maintained around one small area at each movement, balance is therefore controllable, and the sequence is quick and easy to alternate. Amazingly, this crawling action is so reliable and stable that it is not affected by adding weights to the baby's body, or by increasing the incline of the surface on which the baby is crawling.

Experiments have shown that with practice and encouragement, babies are able to crawl up surfaces sloping by as much as 70 degrees.

Early movements

Although your newborn as early as two weeks of age may make crawling-type movements—as when she manages to creep along her mattress—these actions are involuntary. They are not purpose driven or organized in any particular way; in other words, they are not a means of locomotion in the way that crawling is. Even belly-crawling, which some babies adopt at about thirty-two weeks, is not characterized by a well-coordinated pattern of movements; instead, it involves a baby combining pulling, pushing, and shuffling of her body using her legs and bent arms to simply propel her whole body along.

The above may be fairly successful, but it is a clumsy way of getting from A to B, nor is it particularly energy efficient—and minimizing the amount of energy needed to produce movement is the primary objective of adopting a particular means of locomotion. This is true not only for humans but for most animals. The main difference between us and other species is that the latter tend to allocate most of their energy to locomotion, whereas humans are designed to conserve as much energy as possible for the activities of the brain. This is why, at each stage of motor development, we select the method of mobility that is the least costly in terms of energy required. Hence, especially young infants do not really move at all. Their bodies are not mature enough to produce energy-saving movement, so they sleep a lot and don't try to move too much. However, the drive to get moving, to become more independent and explore the world, is strong.

As your baby's muscles grow, and her coordination and ability to learn improve, she will increasingly strive to support her own bodyweight and propel herself forward—or backward, as is often the case at first.

Starting to crawl

How might your baby start to crawl? She could be sitting and playing happily but may drop her toy slightly out of reach, lean forward to retrieve it, and end up on all fours. Alternatively, she may push herself up from the prone position. Either way, she will suddenly find herself in an interesting new posture that prompts her to test the potential of this position by rocking and pushing with her arms—little experiments designed to propel her forward that instead result in thrusting her backward. At this stage, the muscles in the arms are stronger than those in her legs, which is why when her arms and legs are both busy trying to achieve movement, she is often pushed in the wrong direction. Once your baby discovers that a series of movements makes her mobile, she will endeavor to reproduce them, and if this happens to put her in reverse gear at first, it may take another chance discovery—"I can go in the opposite direction if I push harder against my legs"—for her to realize how to propel herself forward. However, the onset of crawling is not just due to strength and strategy. Interestingly, research shows that the ability to stabilize one's gaze while the head moves forward or backward is also crucial to the onset of mobility.

Babies have different styles

Not all babies crawl on all fours. Some save themselves for the even more energy-efficient means of locomotion—bipedal walking—and go straight from sitting to cruising. Those who never adopt hands-and-knees crawling (12–18 percent of babies) may find other solutions to get from A to B before they are ready to stand. They may bottom-shuffle or bear crawl (with hands and feet on the floor, bottom in the air). The latter can result in surprisingly speedy movement, although neither of these alternatives can match regular crawling in terms of efficiency, stability, and versatility. A good means of locomotion needs to be adaptable, because even the home environment is full of surprises, from changing

surfaces (resistant carpet versus slippery flooring) to changing gradients, from obstacles, such as furniture, that need to be avoided to those that must be scaled, such as steps. The hands-and-knees crawler will find it easier to adapt her locomotion to all kinds of different situations than the belly or commando crawler.

Whatever type of locomotion your baby opts for, it will give her a new sense of freedom. Like sitting, crawling isn't simply a motor achievement—it also represents a significant step forward in intellectual development. In becoming independently mobile, endless new possibilities for exploration and discovery open up. Crossing the room one way, your baby will build up an internal map of her surroundings. When it's time to turn around and return to her starting point, she will realize that there are a number of alternative routes from which to choose, giving different perspectives on the room. By being able to move around freely, she can create alternative mental images of the same space. Spatial coordination and understanding develop significantly as a result of the onset of crawling and this, in turn, leads to the emergence of new knowledge and understanding about depth, distance, the properties of different surfaces (slippery, rough, smooth, sticky), and daily dangers that may be lurking around the corner. In fact, the crawling experience has such an impact on a child's understanding of her physical environment that it can be used as a predictor of how she will cope with new challenges.

A baby new to crawling, for example, will probably misjudge her ability to crawl up or down a slope; she will attempt slopes that are too steep and fail to complete the task. Similarly, she will approach a visual cliff (an apparent drop in the transparent surface she is crawling along) without fear. However, within just a few weeks, her experience has taught her both the limitations and versatility of crawling, and she will be able to judge accurately which gradients are safe and what depths should not be crossed. This knowledge is only useful for a short while, for as soon as your baby begins standing up, she will have to learn all over again the whole range of pitfalls and obstacles present in the environment that await her first steps.

Standing up and cruising

Any time from seven months onward, your baby will probably enjoy getting up on her feet from the sitting position when you are holding her tightly under the arms or by the hands. By nine months, when her legs are strong enough to lever her up and support her weight, she may begin to use available supports—other people's legs or knees, handy pieces of furniture—to haul herself into a standing position. At this stage, however, her legs are still only about one-third of her body length, compared to adult legs that account for about half of total height. So standing for any length of time, even with support, requires a lot of muscle power, coordination, and mental determination. In addition to this, your baby faces the problem of how to get back down onto her bottom. Moving from a sitting to a standing position involves a gradual and controlled shift of the body's center of gravity. The inverse action is much more difficult to control, with a precarious moment when balance is tipped far enough downward and rearward to complete the sitting motion. For the baby who is new to the standing game, crash-landing or staying upright until help is at hand is often the only way to get back onto her bottom. This is when diapers really come in handy as padding for a soft landing.

Standing up opens a whole range of new opportunities for your child, such as climbing onto seats and couches, and discovering and reaching for things that were previously out of reach—way above her head. For several months, however, she will not attempt to stand unsupported for more than a brief moment. She can sense that her weight is not stable on her tiny legs and her feet aren't yet reliable bases. It'll take a few months before your baby feels really stable in the standing position. In

the meantime, she will enjoy exploring her environment on all fours. However, the drive to become bipedal is relentless, prompting your child to practice standing at every opportunity. Cruising is just around the corner.

Cruising involves moving sideways like a crab. Because it relies on the hands as much as the feet, it is almost like a vertical form of crawling. Getting from A to B on two feet, as opposed to hands and knees, involves a surprising amount of extra coordination and muscle power. Cruising is a good starting point, because it makes use not only of the legs, but also the strength of the arms to balance and pull the body along. Usually, a baby also rests her chest or the sides of her body against a supporting surface, so that when one leg is off the ground she can retain the upright posture with her body resting on a support. Watch as your baby cruises along the couch; she'll rest her chest on the cushions as she moves. With time and practice, the amount of leverage your baby uses to move along will decrease until the day when she finds herself standing at the edge of a gap between two pieces of furniture and realizes that it's time to let go and step out alone.

Not all babies go through a cruising phase. Some prefer to face the challenge of walking unsupported as soon as they feel confident standing.

Those who do choose to cruise generally begin doing so sometime after nine months. As a means of getting about, it has serious limitations. For instance, cruising consists of moving one limb at a time whereas, as we have seen, crawling involves an optimal pattern of movement using diagonal pairs of limbs. Furthermore, while the support from furniture can run out, the floor surface generally does not. When cruising, your baby is faced with a real dilemma about how to get across gaps between objects to cling onto. This is all good exercise for the brain, however, because it requires your baby to work through a number of options that take into account distance and size relationships, not just between objects themselves but in relation to her own body. Many babies solve the problem of crossing gaps by resorting to a previous means of locomotion—crawling or bottom scooting. Interestingly, they will usually make use of these established skills only long enough to reach the next prop and begin cruising again, although to continue crawling would be far more efficient—evidence, once more, of the irrepressible human drive to walk.

Going up and down stairs

While all babies normally learn to roll over, sit up, reach, and walk, the timing of these and other milestones is to some degree dependent on how much they practice each new action. So children who live in homes with stairs will generally learn to climb them somewhat earlier than children who don't have access to steps. Most babies learn to go up stairs at around ten-and-a-half months of age, after several weeks of crawling experience. However, those who practice regularly may learn a few weeks sooner. Interestingly, this isn't the case for descending stairs. A study found that regardless of the amount of practice available at home, most babies do not attempt to go down steps until around twelve-and-a-half months of age, and most will do so having devised a descent strategy involving turning around and backing down stairs. Descending steps, like sitting down, involves propelling the body in the direction of the pull of gravity instead of against it. It also entails gauging depth and gradients that are more precarious and risky than when ascending.

EVERYDAY MOTOR SOLUTIONS

With so much happening during the first year of life, it's easy to focus on prominent motor milestones at the expense of less conspicuous day-to-day achievements. The amount of skill, judgment, and effort required to climb and descend stairs, for instance, or to pick up a tiny pea or raisin with the thumb and index finger, is commensurate to many of your baby's other triumphs of coordination. Like all early development, however, both are affected by child-rearing practices.

Parental influence—the strategies you teach your baby and the warnings and encouragement you provide—has an effect on how quickly a new skill will be mastered. Without even realizing, you will react to every action, sound, and facial expression your baby makes and, in turn, your child will monitor your responses and react accordingly. This continual interaction provides a scaffold for learning. However, it also puts limitations on your baby's behavior. Your warnings signal danger, while teaching a skill one way may curtail other strategies being developed, and so on.

second stage

Even your attitudes to gender differences can affect how you perceive and respond to your baby's motor progress. One study found that carers of baby boys tended to overestimate their infants' crawling ability, while carers of baby girls underestimated it. This might then be reflected generally, with parents of sturdy boys being more inclined to let their crawlers take more risks, and parents of dainty girls being more cautious, which in turn will affect the children's own behavior.

first stage

The pincer grip

The development of the fine pincer grip—picking up small objects with her index finger and thumb—will be affected by how much practice and experience your baby has at holding and handling toys. At around six months of age, she will begin attempting to pick up small objects that capture her attention. Although her hand-to-eye coordination is fairly well developed by this stage, control over fine motor movements of her fingers and toes is far from perfected.

Initially, she will try to scoop up little objects by pushing them with the side of one hand onto the open palm of the other. This is an ingenious solution to the limitations of her manual abilities, but it does not allow for her to properly inspect her catch. It isn't until she's about nine months of age, around the time when your baby starts using her index fingers to point at things, that she will attain complete finger prehension—the ability to control one finger at a time and use the thumb independently to oppose that finger—allowing for her to develop a neat pincer grip. Total finger prehension is an exclusively human characteristic. Even our clever cousin, the chimpanzee, can at best use only the opposition between his thumb and the rest of his fingers all together to make a pinching hand shape. However, if your baby rarely has access to small objects, she will have less opportunity to perfect this new form of grasping, so once again, parental input will make a difference.

Increased precision

The development of the pincer grip is an important motor milestone, because it provides your baby with dramatically increased precision when using her hands. Small items will hold a new fascination simply due to their previously unattainable quality. This type of play is not simply a fruitless pastime. Through hours of practice picking up little objects, your child will develop increasing confidence in making precise movements and will also learn to discriminate between small changes in objects' sizes, shapes, and weights. Studies have shown that the development of the pincer grasp goes hand in hand with the growth of more mature intellectual achievements. Babies start to be able to select the most appropriate grip for a given situation and to adapt their grasp to special circumstances. For example, experiments have indicated that babies of eight or nine months, who normally have good finger-and-thumb abilities, will resort to other, less mature ways of grasping if the small object (in this case a single Cheerio) to be picked up is on an unstable surface, such as a wobbly tray. This is not the case a few months later. By the age of thirteen to fourteen months, babies have worked out not only how to pluck something easily, but also how to do so without disturbing the balance of the surface upon which the object rests, and will then confidently pincer-grasp a single Cheerio from the wobbly tray.

Safety first

Once your baby has developed the pincer grip, you must be extra cautious about what is left within her reach. Make sure that pills, beads, and, in fact, anything small enough to be swallowed, is kept safely locked away before she reaches this stage. Access to small, safer things, such as raisins, peas, cereal, or cooked rice should always be supervised. Electrical outlets should be covered up, because they may appear inviting to your baby looking to bury her now-mobile little fingers into all kinds of gaps. When outside, watch out for unsuspecting little insects being plucked off the ground to be plunged into baby's open mouth.

Coordinating two objects

You probably won't notice the first time your baby brings two toys crashing together, unless the colliding objects happen to be pieces of your favorite china, of course, but for your baby, it is an important step forward.

Although this new game may seem nothing more than a novel way of making a loud noise, by investigating how objects affect one another, your child has made the crucial initial step toward tool use.

Indeed, once she is able to sit and grasp properly, your baby will spend a lot of her playtime manipulating toys and other objects left within her reach. In particular, this process involves discovering what happens when one object is brought in contact with another or with the floor, the wall, or her own limbs. Banging a toy drum or saucepan lid with a wooden spoon, for instance, will produce a different sound than if she uses a metal spoon. Rapping teddy along a xylophone will not make nearly as much noise as using the stick that the toy came with. All these discoveries will be fascinating to your baby. She will come to understand that certain types of objects are made of material that resists impact, while others cave in, can be compressed slightly, or squashed flat. The same investigation will then lead her to discover that using a rigid object to hit a ball propels it farther than batting it with her soft, bendy fingers. Progressively she will build up mental representations of the different properties of objects and how they behave.

Bringing two handheld objects together is another important step in tool use. It is a more difficult task and involves different dynamics than hitting one object on a solid surface. Your baby has to learn to coordinate the movement in each of her arms and hands simultaneously and judge the distance, trajectory, and speed of both objects. This doesn't simply involve good hand-to-eye coordination. Her posture plays a significant role, too. Babies do not attempt to coordinate two objects until they can confidently sit unsupported, not only freeing their hands but also allowing well-controlled movement of the whole upper body.

Once she has discovered about impact, your baby will try other ways of coordinating the objects she is holding. She may attempt to fit one into the other, attach them together, or place them alongside one another to compare their dimensions; she may pile them up to try to make a tower and then push them slightly to watch them fall. All these actions represent little lessons in physics. Construction toys or jigsaw puzzles that encourage your child to fit certain shapes into different holes will now begin to have a special appeal. You can also try giving your baby a set of different-size plastic containers or other safe kitchen utensils that can fit together, make noise, or act as construction toys.

Learning to use tools

It is important that you keep on the alert for the onset of tool use—not only because it shows your baby at her most ingenious, but also because it may increase the risks she takes, which may place her in dangerous situations. Babies and toddlers naturally grow more inquisitive by the day. With age and experience, they become increasingly creative in their use of objects, actively looking for their hidden potential. From twelve months onward, young children develop a new fascination for buttons, knobs, dials, and switches, anything that sticks out of machines, lights, faucets, and the like. At first, your baby may simply bang these interesting protrusions with her hands. Such early actions are investigative and your baby may show considerable surprise when her behavior results in turning on the radio or turning off the light. Quickly, however, your baby formulates intelligent associations between actions and outcomes, and realizes that to make one object do what she wants, she will have to make use of another. The use of objects as tools now becomes a means to an end instead of simply an end in itself. This means–ends analysis is important, because your child will discover that by using tools she can greatly expand her ability to control her environment.

Sometime between nine and ten months of age, babies begin to understand that acting on one object can affect another. In a series of well-known experiments conducted many years ago, ten- to twelve-month olds were presented with a toy placed on a cloth in the center of a table. While the toy itself was out of the baby's reach, the corner of the cloth was easily within grasp. Even at ten months, before most of the infants could stand, let alone walk, they were already able to work out that by pulling on the cloth toward them, the toy would be brought within reach—knowledge that never goes to waste with inquiring little minds (see also page 154). Within just a few weeks of the onset of crawling, you will find your little one getting in increasingly difficult situations involving an increasingly more diverse range of objects. This is definitely the time for you to become especially vigilant and crank up household safety.

One of the first manifestations of everyday tool use is when your baby uses one object, such as a hairbrush or rattle, to reach another, for example, a ball left on a chair out of reach. This type of behavior involves not only a significant amount of smart planning but also an understanding that one's reaching power is improved by holding and guiding a long object as an extension of the arm. Your child must, therefore, be able to give the object a new, temporary and symbolic identity to fit that particular situation. This is why tool use is often closely related to developments in pretend play. However, using objects as tools is difficult. Although your little one may have realized that an object (a key, for instance) has a function, she may make erroneous assumptions about the nature of that function. So Although she may correctly understand that a key is necessary for opening a door, she may not know how or why. She may spend a long time pulling the key in and out of the lock before, and perhaps simply by accident, turning it to discover how the door finally opens.
So experience as well as a certain degree of chance, and even luck, will be responsible for your child's success in using objects as tools. Imitation will also play an important role, because it is often by watching the actions of others that children are alerted to an object's full potential.

From first steps to striding out

You will never forget the first time you see your baby take an unsupported step forward. Her initial steps may be sporadic and wobbly, but they are, nevertheless, a momentous achievement. This is the moment when your little one becomes a toddler and leaves her babyhood behind. However, while starting to walk seems like the pinnacle of all motor achievements, it actually represents a paradox in development; in giving up crawling in favor of moving upright and on two feet, your baby swaps an efficient, speedy, and safe form of locomotion for an initially slow and hazardous one. Yet, the drive to walk ultimately wins out, in part due to a natural instinct for walking and in part also in response to the reception that walking gets from you and other onlookers. Your baby senses her audience's enthusiasm, feels a real sense of having achieved something special and rewarding, and strives to walk again and again, regardless of how many falls and crashes she has to endure.

Starting to walk

The road to bipedal walking is a long and complicated one, full of obstacles and puzzles for your baby to solve. It requires patience, strength, and determination.

Preparation for walking begins in the uterus when the fetus first starts to make kicking movements. As discussed on page 88, one of the most noticeable reflexes at birth is the stepping one. Although this action involves the same body parts and muscular structure as proper unsupported bipedal walking, at this early stage, a newborn is completely incapable

of achieving balance or supporting her weight. All her muscles are in place, but they are weak and undeveloped, and the "steps" she takes are involuntary reflex actions over which she has no control. However, scientists have shown that these newborn walking movements, and other ones while lying down just kicking the air, are important for future walking.

From around eight weeks, most babies give up "walking" when held upright and instead let their legs dangle limply. It is thought that as a baby grows, gaining fat at a significant rate, her legs become too heavy to lift when in an upright position (bending and straightening the legs from a horizontal posture is much easier, which is why babies practice their kicking when they are lying down, sitting, being held, or in the bath). Gravity is, therefore, the main culprit in bringing about the demise of the walking reflex.

This theory has been confirmed by experiments in which newborns had little weights attached to their legs. The extra weight caused a dramatic reduction in the walking reflex. Similarly, an increase in the frequency and vigor of the reflex was found in older infants when they were submerged up to their torsos in water, surmounting the gravity problem. However, this is not the end of the story. Experience also plays a role in the maintenance and development of certain motor behaviors, including the walking reflex.

Studies have shown that in some cultures where walking is highly valued and actively encouraged from birth, the stepping reflex tends not to disappear at two months, but continues until the emergence of unsupported walking at the end of the first year. However, there is no long-term advantage in speeding up motor development in this way. Data indicate that these early walkers turn out to lag behind in developing other skills less highly valued by their cultures, such as early head control and crawling. So extra practice on one skill may have only local effects and actually slow the baby's progress in other areas.

The age at which babies take their first tentative steps varies dramatically across individuals. Some infants may bravely step out unsupported as early as 11 months, while others prefer to play it safe and wait until they are fifteen or even twenty months. Whatever her age, a baby needs to take her time to develop enough strength, confidence, balance, and mental coordination before she feels ready to walk. Learning to move, after all, is about learning to learn. So, before she can walk, your child needs to have accumulated enough knowledge and experience—about the environment, her body, her abilities, and limitations—as well as muscular strength and coordination to be in a position to let go of support and step out alone.

Walking involves many challenges, the prime one being to stabilize the body on one leg while simultaneously destabilizing the center of gravity and thrusting forward with the other. In taking a step, your baby actually has to push the ground away with one leg, in the opposite direction to the one to which she is actually heading. This has to be done with the correct amount of force so that she doesn't lose her balance while her center of gravity is transferred smoothly from one foot to the other to complete the step. In doing so, she creates a momentary imbalance; at the point when her center of mass has been propelled ahead of one leg, the other leg is being swung forward to support her body and move her on. Faced with such a complicated task at each step, it isn't surprising that your baby requires weeks of practice before she is able to make more than two or three wobbly steps.

Different ways of walking

To overcome the difficulties of walking and keeping balance, babies adopt clever, albeit quirky, strategies. Some hold their arms out above their heads as a counterbalance and proceed with their legs wide apart and feet turned out, waddling from one leg to the other in what is sometimes referred to as the "Charlie Chaplin" gait. They take small variable steps and land flat-footed, and they are forced to recover their balance at every step.

Crashing to the floor is very much part of this experience. In fact, learning to walk is also very much about learning to fall and learning from falling. It is for this reason that you need to be especially careful about where and when you let your baby try out her wobbly steps. You must manage her early walking practice to minimize risk and prevent adverse outcomes. This will give your infant added confidence and bolsters her desire to perfect her new skill. Amazingly, once walking is established, your toddler will take more than two thousand steps and fall about 15 times per hour. This may not sound impressive until you realize that this equates to traveling the distance of more than seven football fields.

Established walking

Your baby's walking will improve relatively quickly, probably because of the sheer amount of practice she will indulge in once she has taken her first steps. As her body thins down and lengthens, the base of support needed by your toddler will narrow, her toes will gradually turn in and point straight ahead, and her steps will grow in length. Longer footfalls will mean that there is more time between one step and the next to calibrate the muscles involved, giving her ankles and knees a chance to flex properly. This means that her steps will no longer end with flat feet, her balance will be more fluidly maintained, and her walking will become increasingly efficient.

Having perfected this skill, your toddler will feel a new sense of independence and you may, as often other parents do, discover the true meaning of the word "tantrum." Your baby's previously beloved stroller is now rejected in favor of slow ambles, your requests to go in one direction instead of another fall on deaf ears, and puddles and mud gain a new appeal.

MORE ABOUT | **EXAMINING DIFFERENT GAITS**

In order to understand how children learn to walk, researchers have examined how toddlers alter their gaits to fit different conditions.

In a series of clever experiments, toddlers were encouraged to descend slopes that varied in incline, and to cross bridges that varied in width and that had either no handrail, a solid hard rail, or a wobbly one. It was found that instead of refusing to complete the task or use previous experience to guide their attempts, toddlers found novel solutions to overcome the obstacles, such as leaning back like a windsurfer and walking sideways along the narrow bridge holding onto the wobbly handrail, or lying down on their bellies and sliding, feet first, down slopes too steep to walk down. So instead of using past experience to cope with new situations—"Last time I went down a slope like that I fell and hurt myself, so I'm going to crawl down this time"—young walkers constantly adapt their locomotion in an attempt to overcome the problem on hand. They may not always get it right, but they rarely give up trying.

THE INDEPENDENT TODDLER

With her new developments in fine and gross motor skills, your toddler is now equipped to become increasingly independent. This is a fact that does not escape her attention; the second and third years of her life are characterized by your baby's growing determination and a stubborn desire to achieve tasks alone. The phrase, "me-do-it," sums it up perfectly, and the best way for you to get through this willful time is to be armed with plenty of patience, humor, and adult self-soothing strategies.

Self-feeding

As soon as your baby is on solid foods, you should begin to encourage her to feed herself. At four or five months of age, she will be too young to manage anything more than the occasional attempt at holding a bottle or grasping a spoon for entertainment's sake. Although the drive for independence is present early on, at such a young age your baby will still enjoy being cared for and pampered by you. However, as she gets older and increasingly in control of her movements, your infant will start to show a strong desire to take over holding her bottle or cup and helping you spoon or smear food from the bowl all over the feeding chair and her face. At around nine to ten months, hand-to-mouth control is being perfected, so your baby may frequently want to take over, but her coordination will still be immature and the success rate for self-feeding can turn out to be minimal.

The best way to encourage your baby to partake in feeding herself is by offering her finger-size pieces of solid foods, such as segments of fruit or sticks of vegetables, pieces of baby rusks and break sticks, or strips of toast. Initially, she may simply play with the food, suck it, squash it, and make a general mess, without swallowing anything. However, all this is good not only for giving her the opportunity to find out about how to feed herself, but also to make mealtimes fun and promote a relaxed and positive attitude toward food. Getting angry at your baby if she plays around when you are trying to feed her can create negative associations between eating and reprimands.

With the increasing social pressures on young children these days to watch what they eat and not to become overweight, you should try to instigate a healthy and comfortable attitude toward food from as young an age as possible.

From the beginning of her second year onward, your baby will start to attempt to feed herself using a spoon. These first clumsy efforts can be entertaining for everyone involved—

although you should arm yourself with a well-stocked pile of bibs, feeding mats, and paper towels. This is clear evidence of tool use. Initially, your baby will grasp her spoon awkwardly, maybe even by the wrong end, and may find it impossible to keep it horizontal, holding it instead as she would a rattle. Thus, it may, at first, be used as more of a noise-making tool than a feeding implement, sending pieces of food flying everywhere, but the experience will not be wasted.

With a lot of patience—from both you and your toddler—and a lot of practice, she will eventually learn to tilt and control her spoon better by using her wrist and adjusting her grip. However, the feeding puzzle is still far from solved. She must now work out how to carefully aim the spoon into the dish so she can fill it with food. This is no easy task. Misfiring with the aim may tip the dish over completely. And even more infuriatingly, it doesn't matter how accurately your toddler manages to land the spoon in the middle of the bowl—it still won't result in her actually getting any food onto it. In order to manage all this simultaneously, she must work out a careful plan of action that involves combining many of the things she would have learned over the past year, including reaching, grasping, and scooping; directing her hand back to her mouth; opening her mouth at the right time; chewing and swallowing; and then starting the whole process again. All these different actions must be carried out in the right sequence and with a high degree of accuracy for any successful eating to take place. Imagine the complex messages that will be sent from her brain to the arms, hands, and mouth. It is easy to get things a little wrong, which is why your baby will seem to find self-feeding somewhat of a struggle and end up with half her lunch on her face and clothes and in her ears and hair. After several attempts, your little one may tire of the feeding implements and resort to the most reliable tool she possesses: her hands.

Interestingly, one of the first indications of whether a baby is right- or left-handed is to observe which hand she will use to pick up a spoon. Research has shown that as early as 11 months of age, a baby will demonstrate a clear preference for feeding herself with one particular hand. Other than this, it isn't

until around two-and-a-half to three years of age that clear-cut handedness can be detected in a child's behavior in activities, such as drawing or hair and teeth brushing.

Drawing and writing

As soon as you notice your child's willingness to use tools, you should start offering her the means to draw. Crayons, pencils, and paper, or chalk and black boards, as independent objects, have little meaning to a one year old. At this age, your baby may show more interest in poking these implements into small gaps, using them as toys, chewing on them, or scrunching up the paper to make interesting noises and shapes. Bringing together drawing tools and paper may not even occur to her. She will still be too young to perceive that combining these objects with hand movements will create interesting marks. With time and experience, however, she will become engrossed in the scribbles her efforts produce and will be delighted by the excitement with which her efforts are received by you. Your encouragement prompts her to draw with even more enthusiasm. Watching a little child draw can be fun. She often gets so engrossed that she becomes oblivious to her surroundings and may even vocalize happily with each hand movement—visible evidence of just how much concentration and brain power it takes to produce even the most rudimentary of scribbles.

As an eager parent, it's tempting to interpret your toddler's early drawings as abstract representations of the world, but, in fact, it won't be until the age of about two-and-a-half years old that your child really begins to attribute meaning to her scribbles. This is often done post factum and it will be hard to know if your child intended to draw a "house" or whether she decided after the event that it was a specific shape, let alone a building. Once the drawing is given a meaning, however, regardless of how little it may resemble the attributed label, your child will stand by that meaning even if you ask what the drawing is a week later.

As your child's representational drawings gradually develop, they may be symbolic in nature, using fixed stereotypical images for things or people. Thus, a person will be drawn as a head with two legs emanating from it; a house may be a pentagon; and a flower, one large circle surrounded by smaller ovals. Surprisingly, these early representations are common among most children throughout the world. They may be a reflection of underlying representational and manual ability. Early drawings will also be almost exclusively two-dimensional, with little attempt to represent depth and distance. By contrast, dimension relationships are apparent at a relatively young age. So daddy will usually be drawn much larger than baby, even if neither actually resembles a father or baby.

By the age of three, your toddler still will not always have a fixed, clear drawing in mind when she sets out to create works of art. Instead, the final creation is often the outcome of one or more reinterpretations along the way. So, for instance, what may start as a person may end up as a sun, or a house might turn into a car. This will be a time when your child will be especially sensitive to the feedback she receives as she draws, and you may find that a comment, such as "Oh, what a pretty flower," may transform the direction of her drawing completely.

Once your young child begins to create meaningful pictures instead of simply squiggles, she also starts to discriminate between writing and drawing. This is not to say that your two-and-a-half year old will be ready to learn to write the alphabet. However she will have been watching your hand actions when you write, she already has an established interest in looking at books and listening to you read the words on the page, and she is now eager to try creating letters herself. She may begin to do pretend writing, and although it may seem much the same to you as scribbling, these efforts will actually be very different from drawing. Unlike drawing, which uses all kinds of different sweeping hand movements while keeping the pencil on the page, pretend writing involves making a series of small marks, sometimes in a tentative line, lifting the pencil off the paper at regular intervals. This may be a good time to introduce the idea of reading, helping her to learn to recognize the shapes of letters and associate them with the sounds they make.

A fully fledged biped

By the time your baby is a fairly competent walker, she will have already mastered stair climbing. Because ascending is far easier than descending, even if she is doing the former upright and on two feet, she may still choose to come down on her bottom. At this stage, walking up or down stairs is done one step and one leg at a time, with both feet coming to rest on each step before the next is attempted. It is only by about 30 months of age that toddlers master the art of stair climbing in both directions with alternating feet on different steps.

By the end of her second year of life, she should be a competent walker, her gait almost resembling that of an adult. Her legs will be fairly close together, toes facing forward, and her arms will swing from side to side close to her body. This means other locomotion will now become possible.

Relatively soon after the onset of walking—about two to six months after the first unsteady steps—your toddler will combine steps in an increasingly fast cycle,

although this is not exactly the same as running, which involves a significantly different set of movements. While walking is achieved by a series of well-coordinated footsteps, running involves a series of well-controlled leaps. Running has what is called a "flight phase," during which neither foot is in contact with the ground.

It is thought that improved coordination alone is not enough to allow for your child to make the transition from walking to running. Instead, scientists believe that changing body proportions, and the ability to send rapid messages from the brain to the muscles, creates the force and motor control necessary to run. Visual processing is also intricately involved, as is head control. For the increasingly mobile toddler, challenges never cease.

Once your baby has learned to walk, new motor skills, such as hopping, standing on one leg, or doing a somersault may go unnoticed by you. However, being attentive to such changes in your baby's movements is rewarding, because every new ability signifies a considerable step forward in your child's development.

About six months after your child starts running, for instance, she should master a series of other movements including galloping, hopping, jumping, and kicking, all the while slowly learning to integrate these varied skills to enable her to dance, take part in sporting activities, or generally entertain you with the energetic antics and daredevil stunts that make the early years such a magical time for everyone.

5

How your baby learns to think

YOUR BABY'S INTELLECTUAL DEVELOPMENT

The early years are a time when your baby's brain is busier than at any other time in his life, developing new circuits while strengthening or pruning synaptic connections (electric currents that pass between nerve cells, which play a key role in the formation of memory). Every sound, sight, and sensation, and each new social encounter that your baby experiences, leads to the strengthening of pathways created in his brain. Learning never stops, not even during the night. In fact, research has shown that much of what your baby learns during his waking hours is consolidated while he sleeps.

Memory and attention are vital to your baby's growing intelligence, too, as is problem solving, imitation, pretend play, and exploration. In this chapter, you will see how your baby uses these skills to take an increasingly active and purposeful role in his expanding world. You will also find ways in which you can both follow your child's progress and help him to make the most of his burgeoning intelligence.

Learning how to overcome ordinary day-to-day obstacles, such as finding a way to get hold of an out-of-reach object, opening a drawer, or balancing one toy on top of another, and other difficult tasks, such as joining in with a game that has a set of rules or grouping objects into categories that will make sense, all involve coordinating different parts of the brain. With so many daily hurdles to overcome, your child's brain is kept busy morning, noon, and night. His intellectual skills are being refined continually, but these improvements may be less obvious to you than his more visible progress in motor development or a growing mastery of language. Looking at the world through your baby's eyes will really help you to help him.

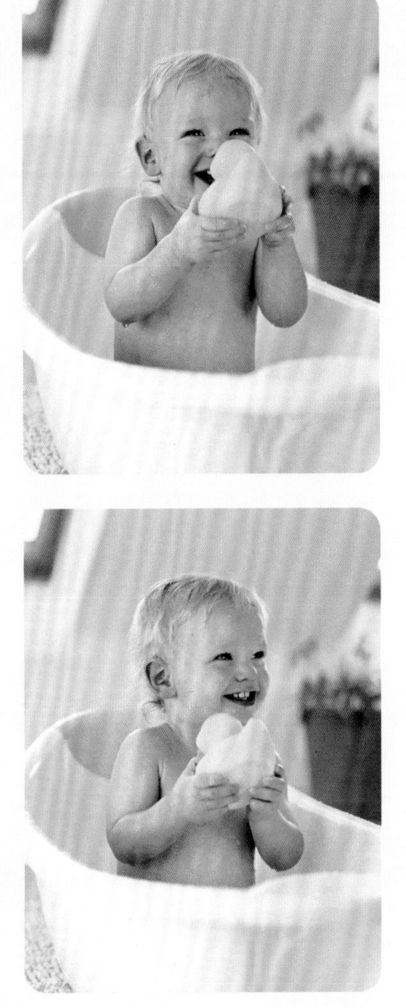

Games you can play

Early learning is something on which you can have a truly positive impact, and providing a stimulating environment—with plenty of opportunities for problem solving, comparing, and categorizing—is a great starting point. If you make sure that your baby engages in simple activities, such as sorting objects by color or size, finds out about the sound and feel of different kitchen utensils, meets other babies in the park, or joins in with preschool music and play groups, you will be providing him with endless learning opportunities. At bath time, when your child dunks different toys under the water, he'll make the surprising discovery that some float while others sink. The law of gravity is nicely tested when your baby watches what happens to the food that gets pushed over the edge of his high-chair tray. Not that such messy habits should be encouraged, but these little experiments all contribute to your child's growing intellect.

Provide love and support

In order to explore his environment and make the most of his experiences, your child needs to feel emotionally secure. Research shows that securely attached, confident children often end up several IQ points higher than those who grow up emotionally insecure. The more confident and secure your child is about your love and support, the more focused and inquisitive he will be about his surroundings. This is particularly pertinent in the preschool period.

During the early years of childhood, when rapid growth and learning take place, your infant's brain is more active and consumes far more energy than in middle childhood and adulthood. During infancy and toddlerhood, both the right and left sides (hemispheres) of the brain are often involved in the processing of all kinds of stimuli—the brain has yet to hone its different areas to specific tasks. Over time, however, areas of the brain begin to specialize, and there is a progressive reduction in overall activity in brain chemistry and brain metabolism. This gradual functional specialization of the hemispheres, which continues throughout the teenage years into early adulthood, is a sign that the brain is becoming more efficient and forming increasingly strong pathways to enable the individual to respond quickly and effectively to new situations and plan his actions accordingly—a final crucial step toward full independence.

Your baby's developing memory

Memory is crucial to almost every aspect of your baby's development, from basic physical tasks, such as learning to move, to complex social conundrums, such as making friends. Although you are often oblivious to the central role that memory plays in governing your behavior, even as an adult, your memories act as pointers, guiding you through multiple aspects of life. The same is true for your little one, although it takes a long time for this infant memory store to build up, and longer still for him to become aware that he has memories.

How memory develops

Memory is the ability to register, retain, and retrieve information about past experiences. We resort to our memories continuously to make sense of events and to predict possible outcomes and interpret new experiences with the help of what we already know. Our memories help us to respond appropriately to what we see, feel, hear, smell, and touch. They not only offer a scaffold for new experiences, but they also represent a store of knowledge that is constantly updated to reflect the changing demands of both our social and our physical environments.

Recall, recognition, and procedural memory

Human memory is a complex system and is largely demonstrated by two processes—recognition and recall. Although they are often confused, they are actually different. Recognition occurs when you remember something as a result of experiencing or seeing it again. Recall, on the other hand, involves accessing from your mind a previously stored memory. It can occur either as a result of a cue (an experience, feeling, smell, or sound that triggers a memory from your past) or it can happen spontaneously (simply remembering something out of the blue). There are two types of recall memory: "autobiographical memory," which includes facts about what happened to you previously, and "semantic memory," which includes specific knowledge that you have about the world (facts, such as "dogs are animals," or "tulips are a type of flower").

You also possess a third form of memory, known as "procedural memory," which includes the ability to recall how to carry out a motor skill, such as riding a bicycle.

All these different types of memory can be held and accessed simultaneously. So, for instance, when your baby crawls across a room, he use of his previous crawling experience to move his hands and legs efficiently (procedural memory); he recalls past events, such as bumping into a wooden chair (autobiographical memory); and he remembers that wooden chairs are hard and couches are soft (semantic memory). Accessing such multiple sources of memory constantly influences your baby's behavior.

How the different types of memory are used

Different pathways in the brain are involved in each type of memory, and every time we remember something, related connections in the brain are strengthened. As a result, memory skills mature at different rates. So an especially young baby, who is still at the mercy of his reflexes, will have fewer autobiographical or procedural memories than a nine month old, who is already actively exploring the world. In fact, for the first two months of life, memory is primarily a matter of recognition. However, it doesn't take long for recall to begin; research has shown that by four months of age, babies display sophisticated forms of remembering.

One recent study showed that if babies as young as four months are shown an object

Human short-term memory is limited. That is why if you're given a telephone number just once, you will usually remember it only long enough to make the call immediately.

In fact, short-term memories, in general, last no longer than a second or two. In order to remember a sequence of numbers, you either have to keep rehearsing it out loud to stop the memory from decaying, or make a note of it for future recall. Information is prevented from fading by being sent to long-term memory for storage. So, writing the number down, visualizing it, or rehearsing it several times, usually means that you are then able to retrieve it correctly at a later date.

Long-term memories are essential for building up a working knowledge of the world, and, in principle, your capacity to store them is unlimited. Factors, such as trauma, illness, and old age can affect the longevity and breadth of your memories, but under normal circumstances, they can last a lifetime.

disappearing behind a screen, they don't anticipate that it will emerge on the other side. However, if they are given some exposure to the object moving along a visible trajectory, they will remember that event and are then be much better at anticipating the object's reemergence from behind the screen, showing that short-term experience is stored in and accessed from long-term memory. This is because the ability to remember entails two processes. The first involves processing an experience in short-term memory. The product of that processing—the knowledge or sensation extracted—is then sent to a long-term memory store, consolidated, and kept for future use (see box above).

Given the right set of cues, recollections of childhood can return to you in old age, bringing with them a mixture of smiles and tears.

MORE ABOUT | **TESTING INFANT MEMORY**

A group of nine-week-old infants was brought into the laboratory and each one, in turn, was placed in a crib with an interesting mobile hanging above it. One of the infant's legs was joined to the mobile with a long piece of ribbon, so that whenever the baby kicked, his or her movements caused the mobile to move.

After two weeks, each baby was tested again, but this time the ribbon was omitted. Despite the time lapse, the babies kicked vigorously, expecting the mobile to move, and showed surprise when it didn't, indicating that they remembered the outcomes of their actions two weeks previously. Curiously, their memories were less good if the designs on the mobile or the crib bedding had been changed, suggesting that they had formed a detailed, context-dependent memory of the total experimental setting.

As with all child development studies, a group of infants of a similar age, who had not taken part in the original experiment, was also tested during the second set of trials to act as "controls" for the experimental group. These babies did not actively kick or show surprise when the mobile remained motionless—an additional demonstration that the behavior of the experimental group in the second set of trials was really due to memory and not just chance.

For your baby, it is only a matter of months before his recollections of favorite toys, family pets, or special occasions will take their place in his long-term memory to form part of what he will one day remember and refer to as his childhood.

Early memories

Your baby's first memories were formed in the womb (see page 12). We know this because infants display preferences for certain sounds just moments after birth. A newborn is attracted to the sound of his own mother's voice over that of other women. Some newborns have even been found to recognize pieces of music that they heard regularly while in the womb through the amniotic liquid. Although it is hard to know the full extent and nature of memories created in the womb and during the first few weeks of life in the outside world, researchers are now devising clever experiments for testing what fetuses and young infants remember. This has allowed us to discover many interesting facts about memory.

For instance, it is clear that babies' memories are initially especially short-lived. In one experiment, three-day-old infants were tested to see how long they could store the memory of a new word they heard repeated several times. Results showed that they were able to recognize it over only one-minute gaps. If playback was delayed any longer, the infants showed no signs of having heard the sound before. At such a young age, long-term memory stores are somewhat primitive, and new experiences can only be encoded at a superficial and temporary level. However, infants' memory skills improve at a fast rate and quickly become more sophisticated. By the time your baby reaches two months of age, he will be able to remember experiences up to two weeks after these occurred (see the box, above).

Early memories are initially context-bound, meaning that recall for past experiences can only reliably occur if the right cues are available. In the experiment described in the box on the facing page, for instance, it was found that certain patterns on the mobile were easier to remember than others: on the whole, crosses were more recognizable than L or T shapes, presumably because intersecting lines are more memorable than two lines that simply meet.

Recall is something that improves rapidly with age. By three months, your infant will be able to form far more coherent, detailed, and long-lasting memories. When the experiment outlined above was done with older babies, they no longer needed a "memory jogger" to remember the mobile test accurately after several days.

Multisense memories

Memories for things experienced through more than one sense—something seen as well as touched, for instance—turn out to be more durable and accurate than those that result from just one form of stimulation—something that, say, was simply heard. This is especially true for babies. So, it is more probable that your infant will remember a new toy that he has been able to handle as well as look at, or a person who stopped to speak to him instead of one who just smiled at him, or a new food that he has been able to smell and touch instead of just taste. Memories are made of pieces of information, so the more details your child can glean from an experience, the more accurate his recall will be. This explains why memory for actions develops faster once an infant is able to take more of an active role in events.

Once your little one is on the move, he will be able to recall his actions far more clearly than when he was stuck in a baby chair watching the world go by.

In fact, from about ten months onward, babies show a clear ability to remember complicated sequences of actions up to one week after having participated in them. For example, if your baby is shown how to construct a rattling toy by placing a coin into a box, closing it, and then shaking the box, he will repeat this sequence several days later when presented with a box and a coin without needing to be shown the actions again. However, if your baby was to simply watch someone else make the rattle in front of him, without being able to try doing it himself, he would not remember how to do it as accurately when given the opportunity at a later date.

By the age of 13 months, a child is able to correctly recall sequences involving up to four separate actions—such as sitting a teddy in a chair, feeding it, putting it to bed, and covering it with a blanket—a week after learning them, even if some of the props are changed (for instance, the teddy is replaced by a doll). This indicates that the memories the babies formed of the original event are coherent, detailed, and flexible enough to be reorganized and adjusted as the need arises. This is absolutely crucial to learning, because one life experience is rarely identical to another.

To progress in the world, a baby needs to be able to flexibly apply what he already knows to changing situations. This is why memory plays such a vital role in your child's developing intelligence.

Remembering encounters with others

Developing memories of people is crucial for your child's understanding of his social world. You have already read how rapidly your newborn stores information about his mother's face, voice, and smell. From early on, the memories he forms also include details about the other people who fill his world. However, how does your prelinguistic child communicate his ability to remember people? One way is by altering the way he responds to different individuals. At eight weeks, for instance, if your baby were to make the acquaintance of a little girl who greeted him by sticking out her tongue instead of saying "Hello," your little one may demonstrate that he remembers this encounter by poking his tongue out the next time the same little girl visits. He's not being rude; instead, it's his way of saying, "Hello again, I've met you before." However, he won't use this form of greeting with other people because sticking out his tongue is a detail that he has attributed to that particular person and is not part of his memories of other individuals.

Using imitative behavior

Imitation is one of the ways your baby can convey his memories before he can speak. So keep an eye open for indications of what he remembers. Pay attention to the things that he directs your attention toward when you visit places. For instance:

- When you return to a friend's house for a second visit, does he look for the cat he met last time or a particular toy with which he enjoyed playing?
- Does he have specific ways of greeting different people?
- When you revisit a place where he heard something frightening, such as a sudden bang or a noisy dog, does he look worried?
- If you've previously played a game at the park or other place, does he demonstrate memory for it by encouraging you to repeat it at your next visit?

There are many subtle ways in which your baby communicates his recall without language, but unless you look out especially for clues, you may miss them. As a parent, you respond naturally to your baby's prompts, often reacting automatically without giving it much thought, so it's easy to overlook the fact that he may not be only interacting but might also be attempting to share a special memory.

Developing memory

A child's memory improves quickly. By the time your child reaches toddlerhood, his recall has become precise—often to a frustrating extent. This is the time when you will start wishing that your child would be a little more forgetful, because toddlers can be fastidious little creatures.

From the age of two years onward, your child, like many children, may start to fixate on things being just so, recalling every little detail of events, so the smallest change to a routine can cause huge tantrums. This will not be the time to try to cut corners when it comes to bedtime stories or games. Your toddler will be keeping close tabs on you: a paragraph missed will probably prompt a request for you to reread the entire page or, better still, start from page one again. As for the loss of a favorite teddy or toy, it is a truly catastrophic even. You won't be able to dupe your little one with a replacement; every detail of the treasured toy—from a crooked stitch to a tiny scratch or missing clump of fur—will have been memorized. In such circumstances, it's probably best to opt for a completely different substitute, one that will provide distraction and for which your child can form a brand-new memory.

GAMES TO ENHANCE MEMORY

There are a lot of memory games you can play with your infant to help bolster his ability to recall.

New and unusual uses

Try introducing your six month old to a new object every few weeks—not just store-bought toys, but safe household items, such as plastic cups or a hairbrush—anything that might be interesting to look at, handle, and bang on the floor. Before handing the object over, show your baby an unusual action with it. For instance, having captured his attention, hold a small plastic cup in your hand and put it on your head several times. Then help him do the same, if necessary guiding his hand and the cup toward his head. Then put the cup away for a couple of days. When you next hand it to him, without doing anything with the object yourself, see if he immediately repeats the action you showed him last time. This would indicate that he has correctly recorded the event in his memory. Don't use an obvious action, such as a drinking motion, because this is what one would normally do with a cup and your baby may be using his general knowledge about cups instead of a specific memory when he recreates the action at a later date. Do something fun instead, such as vocalizing into it or using it upside down as a little drum.

Hiding games

Other games that develop curiosity, recall, and intelligence involve hiding objects. Place a few colored plastic cups upside down and hide a small object under one of them. Encourage your six-to-eight month old to lift the cups until he finds the object. Hide it again under a different cup and make the game more fun by naming the object and asking him where it's gone. This will not only encourage his memory for location but also for object words.

Once your child is crawling, you can play more complicated hiding games involving recall not only of objects but also of different locations around the room. And don't forget to try out the little self-recognition experiments described on page 32—testing your child's response to his mirror image. These can be a lot of fun for you both.

The development of the different senses

Your baby's senses, particularly vision, hearing, taste, and touch, are vital to the development of his intellect. He will use his different senses to gain information about the things with which he comes into contact and coordinate the information to create detailed mental images in his long-term memory that will enable him to take an increasingly active role in daily life.

Vision

Visual acuity, or the ability to bring things into focus, develops rapidly during the first few months of life in the outside world. Improvement in the sense of sight depends mainly on maturation of the eye and visual cortex (an area of the brain involved in processing information from the eye), and although focus improves significantly during the early weeks, it actually takes years for the eyes to mature fully and reach adult levels of acuity. A baby born prematurely will have more experience of the visual world than a full-term newborn, yet despite this extra experience, the premature baby's visual acuity does not improve faster. This suggests that brain maturation also plays an important role in the development of this particular sense.

How vision develops

Your newborn's vision is limited. At birth, he was extremely nearsighted—able to focus on objects only 8–10 inches away from his face (see page 10). Perfect sight is called "20/20 vision," but a typical newborn's vision is only 20/500. This means that the tiny infant has a focusing distance of only 4 percent of that of adults. By six months, this has improved to 10 percent (or 20/200), and by twelve months, to 20/50. This last is approaching adult levels, but it will take another three or four years for your child's vision to reach its full potential. Of course, visual acuity differs significantly between individuals, and some infants may grow to need eyeglasses.

Eyesight is generally tested in the preschool years by means of letter recognition. Your baby's general vision is checked at birth and again by your healthcare provider at his regular developmental checkups. These "tests" take the form of matching games and are based on your child's ability to simply compare the shapes of letters and objects. Even if he tests "normal," if at any time you notice that your baby is squinting (eyes not moving together), it is worth bringing this to your healthcare provider's attention, because the earlier eyesight problems are corrected, the better.

Although all the cells needed for processing and learning are present in the brain at birth, the network of connections linking them is mainly built up during postnatal development. In the visual cortex, for example, specific cells detect edges, straight lines, contours, bars, angles, and contrasts, and your newborn initially responds better to details in his visual environment that are processed by the firing of these single cells. This means that he will be attracted to patterns of high contrast (black and white) and well-defined shapes and large patterns with sharp edges. Furthermore, before the age of three months, your infant can't discriminate all colors. Studies show that he will prefer long-wave colors, such as red and yellow, over short-wave colors, such as blue and green, and will always be more attracted to colors than gray tones. Traditionally, soft pastels are associated with babies but, paradoxically, these are precisely the

If it is visual stimulation you want to provide, always opt for bold colors and patterns when choosing items for your child's nursery.

colors that are far less interesting and appealing to infants. Babies favor garishly colored toys.

Initially, when your newborn scans a stationary object, he first concentrates on one part of the contour. For instance, if he is shown a square, he may fixate on just one corner of it and would, therefore, have difficulty differentiating a square from a triangle (whereas he has no problem seeing the difference between a square and a circle). By six to eight weeks of age, however, he will be able to scan the whole of the contour of a shape. By this stage, he'll also begin to pay more attention to internal details.

After three months of age, his visual scanning will become more integrated, so that he takes account of both the contour and the internal details, which enables him to build a more complete representation of an object. This coincides with his having achieved better head and limb control and is, therefore, a time when your little one is beginning to take a much more active role in what's going on around him, as well as starting to take an interest in toys that are shown and handed to him.

Importance of size and shape constancy

Vision entails far more than simply bringing objects into focus and building representations of what they look like. It also involves an understanding of "size and shape constancy". You instinctively know that things look bigger when they are close by and smaller when they are far away but that they haven't changed size. Likewise, when you rotate an object, its shape seems to alter, but again you know that the object's shape has actually remained constant. Incredibly, your baby's visual system processes size and shape constancy accurately right from birth. Research shows that although the optical image on an infant's retina of an approaching toy gets bigger and bigger, even newborns know that the toy neither grows in size nor changes shape as it moves closer. In one experiment, newborns were shown an image of the same object again and again until they got bored. Next, they were either shown the same image again, but with the object appearing much closer to them, or the image of a different object that appeared the same size. They looked much longer at the image of the new object, which shows that they found it more interesting. This suggests that although the old object had changed size on their retinas, the babies were sensitive to the fact that it was the same object—it just looked bigger.

MORE ABOUT **STEREOPTIC VISION**

You can experience how your two eyes integrate what they see into a single image by looking at the picture of the flower shown here with one eye closed, then the other eye closed, and then opening both eyes to see how the two images merge into one. Because each eye is seeing the picture from a slightly different angle, the visual system calculates the distance from the eyes to the picture.

GAMES TO STIMULATE VISION

Because of the way vision develops, the things that attract your baby's attention will change; the importance of bold colors and patterns has already been touched upon and, by three months of age, your baby will also attend to differences between sharp and gradual changes in luminance, which helps him gain information about the form of objects and where they are in space. So if your house has dimmer switches, you can attract your baby's attention and provide an interesting experience by changing the lighting in a room. Your baby will also be particularly stimulated by moving objects, so instead of simply showing him a new toy or object, you can bring it to life by adding motion.

Prior to the onset of stereopsis, infants use what is called "motion parallax" to gain extra cues about distance and depth. Moving the head slightly causes objects nearby to appear to move more than those farther away. This provides useful information about the location of the object in relation to your baby. You may notice your little one moving his head when he is trying to focus on something interesting.

Test this by playing the following little game. Place two fairly large objects on a table, one within his reach and the other several inches farther behind. Sit your baby on your lap facing the objects and watch whether he moves his head slightly from side to side as he takes them in. If he does, he is using motion parallax to ascertain which of the two objects is reachable. However, if he doesn't make these movements spontaneously, move his head slightly from side to side yourself, and then see if he makes the correct distance judgment by trying to touch the object that is within reach.

Depth and distance

Although size and shape constancy are present at birth, knowledge of depth and distance is not. This develops progressively as a result of both experience and changes in the structure of the eye. The principal clue available to the eyes for judging depth is stereopsis, or stereoptic vision—the process of integrating into a single image what each of our two eyes sees. Adults do this automatically, but babies don't develop stereoptic vision until they are about four months old. However, this doesn't mean that infants see only two-dimensionally. Prior to the development of stereopsis, the visual system will obtain other three-dimensional cues from shading and texture and from the movement of the head, which changes the visual angle on an object and helps the brain to ascertain a certain level of distance and depth information. Yet, stereopsis is crucial for development because it provides the brain with a much faster and more accurate impression of depth than do these other visible clues. Indeed, stereoptic vision is linked to the onset of accurate reaching and tracking of objects—skills that are vital for exploring and learning about the world. Interestingly, children develop this at slightly different times, and girls tend to achieve stereoptic vision about a month before boys.

Hearing

Unlike the sense of sight, the human hearing system is almost fully developed by the end of gestation. From his sixth month in the womb, pathways in the auditory cortex of your baby's brain were already forming. By the time he is born, his hearing has many of the complexities characteristic of an adult's auditory system. This is why, from the moment he enters the world, your newborn is already able to respond to a wide range of sound frequencies (pitch) and intensities (loudness), although his ear canals were initially still full of amniotic fluid. The fluid drained out during the first day of life and then his hearing ability improved considerably. All newborns are given a hearing test; see page 134.

Learning from sounds

Amazingly, the human ear has receptors that can detect sound frequencies ranging from about 15 to 18,000 vibrations (Hz) per second, which allows us to make fine auditory discriminations, essential for speech perception. Of course, our hearing system is not as fine as that of some other species. Bats, for instance, can detect frequencies as high as 100,000 Hz, but they use sound alone for their navigation; humans don't.

Experiments have shown that newborns discriminate between certain sounds better than others: they find it easier to process white noise and pure tones than other more complex sound patterns. White noise is like the sound you hear when a radio is not tuned, when all the sound frequencies are equally intensive, whereas pure tones are simple auditory structures, such as each single note produced by a flute. Although these sounds are easiest to process, newborns still show a strong preference for the human voice, a sound that is, in fact, complex (being made up of multiple frequencies and intensities). This is because human speech is rewarding. So, too, is music, which, like language, follows certain rules, rhythms, and patterns. Combining the two is particularly attractive to infants, which explains why an upset baby is often soothed by the sound of music, especially if his parent is singing along. Scientific data support this. Studies have shown time and again that fractious infants respond far better to sound stimulation—lullabies, reassuring words, or the beating of a metronome—than to silence. Parents and carers automatically use sound to attract a baby's attention; you talk, sing, and vocalize to your infant constantly when you tend to his needs, snuggle with him, or put him in his crib for naps.

Due to your young infant's limited visual capacity and manual coordination, during his early weeks, he spends much of his waking time attending to the sounds that fill his environment—voices, objects rattling,

In the past, hearing problems often went unnoticed until the age of three or four, when children were tested prior to starting school. Clinicians do use the startle reflex (see page 15) to measure responses to sudden sounds, and head-turning and changes in sucking rate can also be used as markers.

Newborn babies are offered either an otoacoustic emission (OAE) test or automated auditory brainstem response (AABR) test. These tests takes a few minutes, are completely painless, and you get the results immediately. In the OAE tests, a small earpiece is placed on the outer part of your baby's ear, which sends clicking sounds down the ear. When an ear receives sound, the inner part, known as the cochlea, normally produces an echo, which is picked up by a machine. In the AABR test, the baby wears earphones and sensors placed on his head measure brain wave activity. In the event of a suspected impairment, additional tests can detect what frequencies appear to be problematic. Hearing tests are important because early intervention can have a dramatic effect, reducing the likelihood of delays in language development and other auditory processing.

telephones, music, cars, the turning of pages, running water, kitchen machines, the unzipping of clothes, and the general hustle and bustle of family life—so his sense of hearing continues to develop at a fast rate, allowing for him to use sound in many useful ways. By listening for voices and movements nearby, your little one is able to orient himself in relation to others. Moreover, as he uses his hearing system to locate familiar voices, he will gradually link his mental representations of these to other details, such as people's gaits, faces, and smells, thereby building increasingly rich mental images of the important people in his life. So the world of sound is a critical aspect of your little one's growing knowledge of his world.

Responding to sounds

An infant's reactions to sound tend to be slower than those of an older child or adult. It can take up to six or eight seconds for a newborn to show an overt reaction to a noise, although his brain begins to process the sound much sooner. This is due to the immaturity of the connections linking different parts of the brain (see page 122). So, in the event of a loud bang, for instance, although your newborn's brain reacted instantaneously to the information, the startle reflex was only evident after a brief delay. The same is true for head turning. You will probably remember how, during his first few weeks of life, your baby took a lot of prompting to reorient his focus toward your face if you called to him when he was looking away. Reactions gradually improve with maturity, so that by the age of about six months, your baby will show much faster behavioral responses to sounds. Despite these early capacities, however, it won't be until he's about 18 months old that your child's hearing system will reach levels similar to those of adults.

Early on, sound is particularly useful for locating objects and people. This is especially useful for your infant, because what he can see is severely restricted by factors, such as posture, visual acuity, and his inability to move around independently. However, what is the true nature of his responses to auditory stimuli?

When your young baby turns his head toward a sound, is he simply acting on a reflex or is he actually turning to look for the object from which the sound emanated?

Researchers continue to disagree on this point, because the latter would involve high-level cognitive processes. To look for the source of the sound, an infant would have to understand that sounds come from things instead of simply responding automatically. However, for familiar sounds, such as his mother's voice, it seems probable that your infant is, indeed, expecting to see you approaching as he hears your voice, and would show surprise (or even distress) if, in the location from where the sound of your voice came, he were to see another female.

At around two to three months of age, there is a tendency for babies to become less automatically responsive to sounds. This is the time when voluntary reactions and movements are taking over from the more reflex-driven ones, and at this stage, there seems to be conflict between letting the body respond automatically to something and choosing how to react. Indeed, many studies have shown that learning to inhibit automatic responses is a clear sign of healthy development. By three to four months of age, your infant will expect objects to make noises and he will become increasingly precise at locating sounds. Research has demonstrated that by this age, he will look more intently at the correct location of a sound instead of just in the general vicinity of the object that made it, and he also will begin to reach toward targets more accurately—his maturing senses prompt him to use his improving motor skills and coordination.

Developmental similarities with vision

The development of hearing and vision share many similarities. For example, like stereopsis (see page 133), whereby each eye provides visual information about depth, each ear also supplies its own information to the brain. The left ear hears a sound at a slightly different intensity to the right, and vice versa. This discrepancy helps the brain to gauge the direction and distance from which the sound emanated. The ability to integrate these two sources of auditory information develops quickly during infancy. By between 16 and 18 months, your baby's ability to discriminate tiny shifts in sound is almost equivalent to that of an adult. So, at this time, if you squeak a toy in a darkened room just in front of your baby's crib and then squeak it again just 20 degrees to the left, he will shift his head a tiny amount to match the new location of the sound.

Receding and approaching sounds

Similar to "shape and size constancy" in the

visual system (see page 131), another auditory skill present in infancy is the ability to discriminate between receding and approaching sounds. By six months of age, your baby clearly demonstrates that he knows, for instance, that the rattle that made a sound nearby is still the same rattle that is making a sound farther away, despite changes in intensity, whereas a different object but with a similar intensity in sound will be stared at for longer.

So, just as with vision, the understanding of sound contributes to your little one's comprehension of the multiple properties that objects can have. This is especially important for learning, because it helps babies build up their knowledge and create rich mental images about the people and objects that fill their world.

Interestingly, if a baby is born deaf, his auditory cortex—the area of the brain dedicated to processing sound—will actually be taken over by his visual processing, demonstrating just how adaptable the human brain can be. For those with visual impairments, similar forms of compensation occur, which explains why the congenitally blind tend to have particularly sensitive hearing (as well as a well-developed sense of touch).

Babies have a "taste" for everything

Mouthing is one of the most noticeable characteristics of infant behavior—no matter how strange or downright disgusting, babies seem to have no hesitation in putting anything and everything into their mouths.

Hand-to-mouth coordination emerges as far back as in the womb, allowing for a fetus to experience tactile stimulation by sucking its thumb. At birth, mouthing occurs as a result of responses to certain smells as well as to touch—both of which can prompt the rooting (see page 13) and sucking reflexes. The hand-to-mouth reflex is a little different, becuase it involves the baby's mouth opening in anticipation of his approaching hand. So it is neither prompted by hunger nor by the face being touched. Research has shown that the presence of a sweet taste in the mouth, such as milk, is accompanied by an increase in the frequency with which babies bring their hands up to their mouths. So, initially, it seems that hand-to-mouth behavior is mainly feeding related. However, mouthing soon progresses beyond this, becoming your infant's prime means of exploring objects during the early months, a time when his hands are still clumsy appendices on the ends of his arms.

"Mouthing" in young babies

During early infancy, there are considerably more nerve endings in the mouth than in the fingertips. In fact, the neural pathways relating to the tongue, lips, and palate are the first to develop in the cerebral cortex, and are, therefore, the most sensitive organs for examining objects. That's why your baby will bring anything placed in his hands directly to

his mouth—not because he wants to eat it but because he wants to explore its properties. Mouthing increases rapidly over the first six months of life. Even prior to the emergence of voluntary reaching, your infant will explore an object placed in his hand by putting it in his mouth. He will do this before either looking at or manipulating it. Through trial and error, your baby soon learns that some objects are more suitable for mouthing than others. For instance, furry, stringy items, such as teddy bears or human hair, are easy to bury fingers into, but not pleasant to fill the mouth with, so these are generally not explored orally. The same is true for heavy and large objects that either weigh too much or are too big to bring up to the mouth (although one way around this problem is to bring the mouth to the object, which is why you will often find your baby mouthing the side of his crib or the edge of his chair). The prime candidates for mouthing, therefore, are smallish (obviously not too small to present a choking hazard), light, solid, or squashy objects. Interestingly, although more or less anything will be mouthed, research has shown that by about four to five months of age, infants tend to mouth silent objects, such as the edge of a plastic plate, more than audible objects such as rattles, which are better waved to create a sound. If given a choice, they seem to work out for what each object is best. This is probably because they are already starting to categorize objects and have realized that certain actions will lead to the discovery of different kinds of information.

Coordinating the senses

Although the foregoing pages look at how the three main senses develop independently, in reality, it is rare for something to be experienced through one sense only. Instead, information from the eyes, ears, fingers, nose, and mouth is combined to build a complex, multidimensional representation of an object, event, or person. This ability to coordinate information from two or more sources is known as "cross-modal matching." It allows for you to use memorized information to compare, recognize, and classify things. In practical terms, it enables you, for instance, to visualize in your mind a person you cannot see but whose voice you can hear, or to identify an object you set eyes on for the first

MORE ABOUT | **WHY BABIES MOUTH**

In the first few months of life, the lips and tongue offer so sensitive a means of exploration that they can provide a baby with an accurate mental image of the object being mouthed, even if the object remains unseen. In one study, two-month-old babies were given either a pacifier with a bumpy teat or one with a smooth teat to suck. The babies were unable to see the pacifier before they were put into their mouths, so the only information they could gain about them was from mouthing. While they were sucking, they were shown two pictures simultaneously: one of the bumpy pacificer, the other of the smooth one. Remarkably, the babies preferred to look at the picture that corresponded to the actual pacifier they were sucking; they had accurately matched and integrated the information obtained from the mouth with that procured from the picture by the eyes.

time but whose sound you have heard before. Your brain performs this kind of cross-modal matching by using the stores of information you have in long-term memory without you being aware that this is going on; it is a skill you take for granted. However, is the ability to cross-match sensorial information present at birth, or is it something that develops over time as a result of experience and maturation?

Cross-modal development

Because many developmental milestones could not be achieved without cross-modal matching, it is apparent that the senses become increasingly well-integrated with age. Yet, the early signs of multisensorial coordination are difficult to see in especially young infants, and they are even more difficult to assess. Newborns have been shown to be able to match the image of two dots on a computer screen when they hear the sound of two drumbeats, but these results are difficult to interpret. Some researchers believe that they stand as evidence of matching across the senses, while others argue that newborns initially have an "amodal" form of mental representation—that is, they can make these links because they represent the information they obtain from each of their different senses into a single, identical, abstract mental image that does not require cross-modal matching. Once infants reach three months and are involved in active and voluntary exploration, it is generally agreed that integration of the different senses and true cross-modal matching play a major role in helping them learn about their environments.

Interestingly, it is not until between four and eight months of age that your baby's fingertips will be sensitive enough for him to be able to equate what he can feel in his hands with what he is looking at (see the box, below). The growing use of his hands as a means of exploration and control over the environment, together with later improvements in locomotion, such as crawling, lead to additional exciting developments in your infant's intelligence. For example, as you saw in the previous chapter, babies moving around independently—be it by crawling, walking, or cruising—learn to cope with different surfaces, slopes, or narrow crossings.

Scientists have also done a lot of research

MORE ABOUT **STUDY TO TEST PERCEPTION**

In one study, four-month-old infants were presented with an object that they could not see but that they could explore with their hands under a blanket. One group of infants was given a pair of rings joined by a flexible string, while the other group was given rings joined by a rigid rod. The difference between the two stimuli was that the first seemed to be two objects that could move independently of one another in each hand, whereas the other formed a rigid, single object. After exploring the objects under the blanket, the infants were shown two visual displays, one containing two rings separated in space and the other containing two rings joined by a straight bar. Once again, these young infants displayed amazing intellectual capacities by looking longer at the display that corresponded to what they had felt with their hands.

In this test, a transparent surface (such as toughened Perspex) is placed over an area of checkerboard pattern made to look as if it has both a shallow and a deep end. Babies are encouraged to crawl over this surface, by their mothers calling them at the other end.

Before the onset of crawling, babies show no fear of being placed (either in a sitting or an all-fours position) on the surface above the "deep end"—perhaps because they are not yet able to properly cross-match what they feel with their bottoms and limbs ("I am on a solid surface") with the information their eyes are providing ("I am positioned above a drop").

However, once babies are able to crawl or bottom scoot across the surface unaided, they display a strong reluctance to cross the visual cliff and refuse to crawl over the deep end. This is still the case if the baby's mother is asked to stand by the deep end and encourage her child to crawl over what actually remains a solid surface throughout.

on infants' reactions to changes in depth, using a method called the "visual cliff." This test indicates there is an age at which the information the baby gets from his eyes ("There seems to be a drop here") overrides the information he receives both from his sense of touch ("This is a solid surface") and from his mother ("It's perfectly safe to advance"). Later, of course, the baby will weigh up the information from his different senses and will listen to the social reassurance he receives to make the well-informed decision that there is no risk in crossing the visual cliff. By this stage, his senses are working together to provide information about his environment and guide his behavior. He is also now able to order this information hierarchically in response to the changing demands of each situation.

Risk assessment *depends on the information a young child gets from her eyes, hands, and feet.*

Making sense of the world

Does your newborn infant intuitively know that the world and everything in it continues to exist while he is asleep? This is a question that scientists have argued over for more than half a century. What is known is that a seven-month-old baby who is busily engrossed in trying to reach an interesting toy placed on a table in front of him may cease his attempts if the toy is suddenly covered with a cloth. This observation originally led psychologists to conclude that during the first year of life, infants have no concept of "object permanence"—they don't know that an object continues to exist when it is no longer in sight. The development of new research methods, however, enabled scientists to challenge this assumption about infants' mental representations. It has now been shown that, under certain circumstances, babies as young as three to four months old, show a sensitivity to object permanence. The problem with the old methods of testing were that they were too dependent on a baby's ability to reach, which, as we saw in Chapter 4, takes some time to occur and to perfect. So, instead, the new research focused on infant "looking behavior," a change that allowed for babies who were not yet able to reach accurately to be tested.

Understanding object permanence

The ability to maintain a concept of an object in space and time, despite its momentary disappearance, is crucial for understanding the way the physical and social worlds behave. Imagine if each time you left the room, your infant thought you had disappeared forever. The fact that your baby can internally form a

MORE ABOUT | **TESTING OBJECT PERMANENCE**

In order to test early sensitivity to object permanence, four month olds were shown a locomotive moving along a track, which then disappeared behind a screen and reemerged on the other side. After repeating this event several times, the screen was removed and, while the baby was watching, a large wooden cube was either placed across the newly exposed part of the track, blocking the train's future passage, or next to the track, leaving the passage free. The screen was now replaced, hiding that part of the track. The train was then made to start its journey again, and in both cases it completed its journey. Babies who had watched the cube being placed across the track showed surprise at the train's successful passage, suggesting that they had expected the hidden cube to block the train. Although they could no longer see the cube once the screen was in place, they nonetheless maintained a representation of the cube and its position and predicted its effect on the train's trajectory. So out of sight is not necessarily out of mind, even at this especially early age.

Gone but not forgotten. *With time, your baby will know that when you leave the room, you haven't disappeared forever.*

mental representation of you, and maintain that representation when you are not present, is fundamental in building up stable ideas about the environment. Such representations may initially be somewhat crude, but they form an important foundation for later intellectual development.

With time, your infant's representations become more elaborate, enabling him to encode especially complex features of events. By seven months, for instance, your baby will analyze objects along many dimensions. He will notice size, texture, shape, and color, and predict the behavior of objects according to specific features. This is important for object permanence. Your baby now not only represents an object as present or not, but is also capable of inferring how it will behave out of sight—that is, he will assume its properties will remain permanent even under different circumstances. So your infant will expect a hard, wooden cube to remain solid, even when hidden by a screen, and will show surprise if the screen drops back and apparently flattens the cube (which, unbeknown to your baby, will have been surreptitiously removed). However, he won't show surprise if a sponge seemingly gets squashed by the screen.

Object permanence also allows for your baby to maintain internal representations about size and shape. This enables him to compare objects out of sight. So, if a marble rolls across the floor and out of view, your infant will expect it to come out again from under the couch. He will expect a bigger rubber ball to behave differently and maybe get stuck under the piece of furniture. Holding information about size and compressibility in mind, your baby will be able to judge which of the two objects will probably reemerge. These examples may seem trivial to you, but they illustrate some of the clever intellectual advances made during the second half of your baby's first year.

By the time he's around nine months old, it will be easier for you to notice your baby's increasingly sophisticated knowledge about objects, which will be clearly detectable in his reaching behavior. For instance, if you hide a toy under a soft cloth, your nine month old will lift the cloth to reveal the toy, but, once he has been successful in finding the toy, he will keep looking under the same spot, even when you visibly move the toy to a new hiding place. This is because, at this young age, your baby still cannot inhibit the earlier successful response he has learned.

It is now known that memory plays a role in an infant's erroneous reaching. If he reaches for a toy immediately upon seeing it being moved, he is more likely to pick the correct hiding place than if he waits several seconds.

As your baby gets older, his memory will improve and he can tolerate longer time delays between hiding and reaching, and, thereby, inhibit his reaching to the wrong hiding place. By his second year, he will not only be able to follow visible displacements, but he will also make inferences about invisible displacements. So, if your toddler watches a hand go into a box where he knows that a tiny toy is hidden, and the hand subsequently moves to another hiding spot, he will immediately look in the new location although he only saw the hand move and not the toy itself. Your toddler will have made the correct assumption that because the toy was small enough to fit into the closed hand, its removal to a new hiding place must have been the aim of the action. This understanding of invisible displacement not only marks the culmination of "object permanence" but also indicates other important intellectual developments. In making the assumption that the toy was moved, your toddler will also have specific expectations about the goals behind the behavior. In other words, your child must integrate some social knowledge about goal-oriented behaviors with what he knows about physical things and how they work; your little one will be cleverly combining all his knowledge to better interpret his exciting world.

Learning about the laws of physics

Getting to grips with how the world of objects functions is one of the vital steps in your infant's understanding of some of the basic physical laws that govern life. One of these principles, for instance, stipulates that a solid object cannot pass through another solid. Your three month old will display his sensitivity to this fact by showing surprise if he sees an on-screen scene that depicts a ball magically passing through the surface of a table. From around five months of age, your baby will understand something about gravity, too. So if you throw a ball from a height and magically stop it midair, before reaching the floor, your baby will appear surprised, because his expectations of the ball falling to the floor will have been violated. By seven months of age, your baby can predict that gravity will have an effect on the speed of a toy car traveling up or down a hill. He will expect the car to roll progressively faster as it comes down, and to go slowly uphill. We know all this because of experiments that monitor minute changes in babies' behaviors in response to either expected or unexpected outcomes.

This knowledge about cause and effect in the physical world is called upon whenever your baby encounters a new situation. It helps him to anticipate, infer, and appropriately respond to novel stimuli or events that require problem solving. If you were to play pool, for instance, you know that the impact of one ball (A) on another (B) will make ball B move. Imagine your surprise if ball B were propelled forward before ball A hit it. Similarly, it would make no sense to you if, upon impact, ball B were to pause for a moment before moving. Infants as young as six months have the same expectations about the outcome of impact between two objects.

Without having seen a cue, much less a pool table, babies will show surprise when certain basic laws of physics are violated. This is because

HOW *you can help*

LEARNING CAUSE AND EFFECT

Although your baby makes inferences about object relations well before the onset of language, these may not be obvious to you. Researchers can demonstrate underlying knowledge through scientific experiments, but unless you actively look for evidence of it in your infant's behavior, the extent of his understanding of the world will remain hidden until he is able to start asking questions and offer explanations.

During your baby's first 18 months, look for little clues to his budding knowledge by observing the way in which he manipulates and plays with his toys, and by noting the things or events to which he wants to draw to your attention:

- Does he test out the same action on a variety of objects or surfaces?
- Is he trying to find something out when he dips his bread into his juice?
- What might your baby infer from squeezing each one of his teddies through the stair gate to see them fall to the floor below?

Being sensitive to your child's inquisitive mind will let you share in his intellectual development. It will also provide plenty of anecdotes to relay in later life—and children love to hear about all the silly things they got up to as babies.

Once he begins speaking, you can follow the development of your child's knowledge even more closely, by listening for subtle changes in his use of words. Most children first produce words referring to objects and people: "mom," "bottle", "ball," or "dog". These are just labels. In order to communicate something about their primitive knowledge of the behavior of things, they need to use action words, too. So, when your child begins to use words such as "gone" or "bye-bye," you can take this as a sign that he is intentionally telling you about his grasp of object permanence and words such as "there" to indicate location. Finally, like some children, your child may use words such as "oh-no" to mark a thwarted problem-solving attempt and composite words such as "got-it" to mark success.

Then, at around two years of age, there will be a change toward expressed curiosity and a thirst for knowledge with the onset of "why?" questions that can be endearing and impressive at first, but after the third or fourth "why" will probably drive you mad.

just by paying attention to what is going on around them, they have come to understand something fundamental about the spatial and temporal constraints that dictate the cause-and-effect relations between objects. In doing so, they realize that these are different from the constraints that operate for living things, such as people, who move of their own volition and can resist moving even when something hits them!

Everyday activities, such as being given a bath or sitting in a highchair, provide your little one with numerous opportunities to make interesting and fun discoveries about the laws of physics. For instance, he will discover that if he drops his hollow plastic duck into the bath, it will float on the surface of the water and will not stay underwater even if he pushes it down to the floor of the bath. A bar of soap, on the other hand, will behave differently.

Your infant can spend hours experimenting, so even if it means some delay in your daily routine, or a mess being made during a meal, do try to encourage his curiosity. Simple little "tests," such as hitting the bath water with different objects to see which of them causes more of a splash, or dropping different objects out of his crib to see which ones bounce, make a noise or roll away, will teach him things that no class in school or book could ever let him discover in such a fun and creative way, or with the same sense of wonderment.

Learning about balance

Through both observation and exploration, your baby will also find out about the principles of balance. Amazingly, your seven month old will be capable of assessing whether one cube placed on top of another will successfully balance, based on how much of the top cube is touching the surface of the bottom one. He will appreciate the relationship between an object's position on a surface and its center of gravity. If, for instance, he is shown on a computer display one cube made to balance on top of another with only a tiny part of their surfaces touching, he will show surprise, indicating that he expects the top cube not to balance but to fall. At this age, however, he will only be able to assess balance relationships of simple, symmetrical objects, such as building blocks. Asymmetrical objects, such as spoons, where one end is heavier than the other, or odd shapes whose centers of gravity are not in the middle, will pose a problem, even when he is nine months old. He won't be able to judge how these kinds of objects need to be placed in order to balance and will show no surprise if an asymmetrical object doesn't fall off a supporting surface when you know that it should. It will take several more months before he will be sensitive to the fact that an object's center of gravity does not always lie above the geometric center of the length of the object. This understanding probably comes from his greater experience in handling and playing with construction toys of different shapes.

MORE ABOUT | **TESTING CATEGORIZATION**

If a one-year-old child is given an array of yellow plastic animals and vehicles to play with, he will examine sequentially all those that belong to the animal category before he starts to explore those belonging to the vehicle category, although, for instance, a plastic bird with outstretched wings looks much more like an airplane than it looks like a dog. In other words, after being given a series of animals, he will suddenly spend more time playing with the airplane, as if to indicate that he is aware that the category has now changed.

What is particularly interesting about this experiment is that the infant is not fooled by perceptual likeness; the bird and the plane look similar but his behavior shows that he knows they are not conceptually similar. So he makes the bird fly, hop along the floor, and chirp, and may even feed it with pretend water, whereas the airplane is held high above the head and made to fly with pretend engine noises or moved along the table like a vehicle.

A one year old will not pretend to feed the airplane or make engine noises for the bird. His distinctive behavior with each toy indicates that he has correctly placed the bird in the animal category and the plane in the vehicle category, despite the fact that the two toys are the same color, size, texture, and general shape.

Learning to categorize the world

It is difficult to ascertain the precise age at which babies begin to organize their knowledge, grouping the things that fill their world into different categories. Categorization is a vital skill that assists learning in many important ways. Most notably, it allows for an infant to accumulate and process information faster and more efficiently. This is especially helpful in new situations, when a baby's senses are being bombarded with information that all needs to be processedfor the baby to assess his surroundings and respond accordingly. By storing information with the help of categories, he reduces the need to relearn things over and over again. Imagine how difficult life would be if, every time you saw a different car, you had to relearn that a car is a vehicle that has wheels, is made of metal, and moves. By creating a category for "car," and a higher level category such as "vehicle," you can keep knowledge of this kind together and use it to analyze all the different large, moving objects you then see every time you walk down a street.

From an especially young age, your baby begins to analyze his environment along several dimensions. At first he will note whether an object is self-propelled or needs to be pushed in order to move, then what type of movement it makes and features such as color, general shape, and texture. These characteristics allow for your baby to form a number of global categories, such as animal, vehicle, or furniture, for instance, within which things can be grouped together. For the animal category, features might include: is self-propelled, has legs, a furry texture, and a face. The furniture category might cover properties such as doesn't move, is solid, can be sat or leaned on, and doesn't make a noise. It is easy to see how your infant's early categories may be somewhat inadequate, but they serve to help him make sense of the world.

Global-level categories, such as animal, vehicle, and male/female form part of your infant's intellectual tools from as early as seven months of age. Experiments have demonstrated that by the second half of their first year, infants are already categorizing objects and animals into two separate groups. This is demonstrated by their being able to discriminate the "odd one out" when shown a series of images of animals interspersed every now and then by the image of an object, or vice versa. Babies look more intently at the unexpected image as if to say, "This one doesn't belong to the same category as all those others." Somewhat later, around 12 months of age, they begin to display this category knowledge in their exploratory behavior (see the box, page 145).

From about twelve months onward, therefore, categorization is based less on salient features, such as shape or color, and more on the meaning or function of an object.

Creating more complex categories

During his second year, your toddler will begin to actively incorporate increasingly detailed criteria to form more complex classifications. The wide category of vehicle will now be subdivided into more precise categories, such as car, flying vehicle, or truck, depending on their different sizes, shapes, actions, and, above all, functions. Similarly, the animal category will be divided into dogs, cats, bears, birds, and so forth. Soon, these will become further refined categories that will differentiate between an German shepherd and a poodle, for instance, or a truck and a bus. Note that it is not that your toddler has

suddenly become able to see the difference between a truck and a bus—he has been able to make this differentiation since early infancy. What has changed through intellectual development is that his behavior is no longer governed by perceptual differences but by classifications based on conceptual differences.

Finally, between 20 and 24 months, the onset of the vocabulary spurt will provide your child with labels for a growing number of his categories, so that he will now be able to communicate to others how he is interpreting and categorizing the world. From this point onward, your toddler will become an avid little "sorter," trying to fit each new encounter into a preexisting category or creating new ones to catalog his expanding worlds.

Learning through play

From an early age, your baby begins to mimic the behavior of those around him. Imitation is not only an important part of social interaction, but also plays a vital role in learning and problem solving, helping your infant acquire knowledge and skills.

Mimicking the behavior of others

Imitation allows your baby to learn new behaviors, which he doesn't produce spontaneously, and also enables him to find solutions when his problem-solving skills or other general abilities let him down. For instance, your infant may watch his dad hammering a picture hook into the wall and then start banging his rattle on the wall in imitation—even though he doesn't understand the function of his father's action. Such mimicking may not achieve much at the time, but it can often lead to fortuitous discoveries. For instance, your baby may discover that banging the rattle against the wall attracts your attention, useful knowledge for next time you ignore him. Alternatively, he may discover that the noise of the rattle when banged against the wall differs from that produced when it is banged on the floor, and so on. So a simple copied action may lead to multiple social and physical discoveries.

Imitation can also provide evidence of your infant's growing theory of mind (see page 42); it indicates new understanding about the relationships between the self and others. By playing peekaboo with you, for instance, your baby shows that he understands your actions, can re-create them himself, and is able to predict that his reciprocal behavior will have a similar meaning to you. In other words, your baby realizes that the game has a goal, involves an element of surprise, and causes the other person to respond. However, this is only part of the picture. The imitation process also involves complex, cross-modal coordination between the pathways in the brain that govern action and those that govern thought. To imitate successfully a much more simple action, such as opening his mouth wide, for instance, your infant has to map the movements he sees on your face onto an action plan that will help him achieve the same motor output on a part of his own face that he cannot actually see.

Imitation, which is rarely if ever seen in other species, seems to be a fundamental learning mechanism in humans.

Accurately copying someone entails complex intellectual and physical processes. Researchers disagree as to whether newborns and especially young infants are really able to mimic someone intentionally or whether they are simply displaying reflexlike behavior when, for instance, a baby puts out his tongue in response to a parent doing so. Amazingly, this imitative behavior can occur only moments after birth. Newborns can also repeat their parents' head movements from side to side. Yet, these actions all form part of an infant's normal behavioral repertoire, and in certain circumstances the same response can be prompted by completely different stimuli. For instance, studies on newborns have also shown that they will probably put out their tongues in response to watching a pen protruding in and out of a tube, indicating that this behavior may be neither social nor volitional. It is only later that a baby will develop imitation by gauging his mother's intentions in doing an act, then trying to mirror these himself. This is because imitating another person's behavior involves progressively recognizing that humans are alike, both in body

and in mind, something that takes time to fathom. For this reason, many scientists argue that newborns lack the higher cognitive capacities required to form the mental representations needed to imitate voluntarily. Having said that, it is still a good idea to play imitation games with your young baby. Poking your tongue out, opening your mouth and eyes wide, moving your head from side to side, and opening and closing your fists, while your baby watches intently, are all actions that will provide exciting stimulation and will probably bring about rewarding interaction. Irrespective of whether these little exchanges involve true mimicking, they help to strengthen connections in your baby's brain, promote close parent–child interaction, and are a lot of fun!

The development of imitation

Imitation progresses through a number of stages. As mentioned above, intentional mimicking is questionable under the age of two months. True imitation emerges once your baby reaches three months of age, and this opens up new opportunities for interaction between you and your little one. Infants tend to copy mostly those actions that they are able to produce naturally in day-to-day life. The farther a behavior is removed from a baby's daily repertoire, the harder it is for him to reproduce.

Take the example of tongue protrusion. Your newborn could imitate this enthusiastically early on—probably because it formed part of his rooting and sucking reflexes. By four months of age, however, your baby is less interested in imitating this gesture because it is being replaced by more intentional behaviors, such as trying to produce babbling sounds and hand gestures. He is now more easily enticed to imitate clapping, vocalizing, or facial expressions that prompt laughter, all of which he can now do voluntarily.

It is not until he is eight months old that your infant really will begin to imitate unfamiliar actions, such as brushing his teeth or spooning food into his mouth. Yet, even at this stage, he needs to have a model to copy to reproduce an action or sound. Delayed imitation won't occur for some time yet. Nevertheless, the first half of the second year of your toddler's life will be generally marked by a growing interest in copying new behaviors. Now, however, your child will concentrate mainly on actions that are pertinent to the situation in hand. He will try to copy any action that might help him accomplish his goals. This is why it can be far more difficult to get your one-year-old baby to clap his hands or wave his arms by request than when he was nine months old. Whereas your nine-month-old infant will find the simple act of mimicry satisfying, once he's a year or so, if he's busy arranging his toys in a line, he will not be interested in interrupting his activity to clap or wave. To encourage him to take an interest in mimicking you, try counting his toys by touching each one in sequence.

By the beginning of his second year, imitation will become not only more complex but also increasingly accurate. Your child will now be able to reproduce a behavior almost exactly as he sees it. This is not only useful for solving problems in the material world but also gives your child the means to safely explore issues involving social interaction, something mainly done through pretend play, which emerges around eighteen months of age. Your child may act out with toys a quarrel he witnesses or an incident that frightens him to make better sense of it, or he might just practice the art of communicating with others by giving his teddies voices and making them play a game he watches other children take part in at playgroup.

It is only by the age of 14 to 18 months, that your baby's memory will be developed enough to allow him to store and then reenact a sequence of actions using just recall—delayed imitation—which will demonstrate how important memory is in play. Now, to accurately reenact something he has witnessed, your child no longer requires an immediate model or practice. This is an important development, because it means that he is now free to revisit situations and test out different ways of responding to them—something that often takes place during those moments when he is busy chatting to himself alone in his crib or on the floor amid his toys.

Learning about numbers

Counting is a skill that is initially learned as a result of imitation. Numbers are the means by which you can quantify the things in your life. They also help you to process, classify, and categorize information that reaches your brain, which is why numerical knowledge is such an essential part of everyday existence. Along with human beings, many other species of animals and insects possess the ability to quantify, which enables members of herds to monitor their numbers and keep track of predators and food sources. Although you may be unaware of their vital role most of the time, numbers permeate almost every aspect of your life, from shopping to judging distances. Without numbers, we would have no way of performing simple tasks,

To discover something about babies' secret knowledge of numbers, scientists have devised some experiments using sucking and looking-time techniques. By recording subtle changes in a baby's sucking rate or the amount of time he prefers to look at one display instead of another, researchers have established new facts about three month olds' understanding of numbers.

At this young age, infants already display strong expectations about what they are seeing or hearing based on their numerical sensitivity. For instance, if infants are shown a series of interesting displays on a computer screen, all containing three items (three flowers, then three cars, then three balloons, and so on), occasionally interspersed with sets of two items (two flowers or two balloons that look the same as the others), they will suck harder on a pacifier or look longer at the screen that shows the unexpectedly reduced number of items.

This ability isn't only restricted to visual stimuli; babies also display early numerical sensitivity to auditory stimuli. Thus, if a baby is played sets of three drumbeats, interspersed with an occasional set of two drumbeats, he will react longer to the lesser number of beats—even if both sets are carefully regulated to span the same amount of time.

By five months, a baby will be able to use his number knowledge cross-modally. This means that he will now correctly match what he hears to what he sees, and vice versa. So, if your baby hears a set of two drumbeats while simultaneously watching a visual display containing either two or three items, he will look preferentially at the display containing the same number of beats he just heard. This shows that your infant can integrate numerical information across two senses. However, this numerical discrimination applies to numbers only up to three or four.

such as working out a baby's age or measuring ingredients while cooking. There would be no understanding of the monetary exchange required to purchase goods or a way of keeping schedules—the world would be chaos.

From early on, quantification plays an important role in the way in which your infant processes his environment. At as young as three months of age, your baby may exhibit signs of a rudimentary understanding of numbers. As you have read in previous chapters, humans are born with a predisposition to attend to complex visual and auditory stimulation. From the moment of birth, your little one's attention was attracted to sights and sounds that contained many interesting contrasts and changes. He quickly learned to discriminate between displays with few details versus many elements. By three months of age, for instance, your infant is able to demonstrate that he has learned to differentiate between groups of one, two, and three objects. He knows nothing about the words "one," "two," and "three" or the symbols that represent these words (1, 2, 3), but he is already sensitive to the fact that a group of three dolls contains the same number of items as a group of three teddy bears. He can also discriminate between one object and a set of two or three objects.

However, at such a young age, your baby cannot tell the difference between sets of more than three items. It seems, then, that early on, a human infant's capacity to process multiples is restricted to amounts of four or below.

By seven months, this will improve so that your baby will now be able to discriminate between larger groups; for instance, he will know that a group of eight items is not the same as one containing sixteen—a ratio of one to two—but he cannot yet discriminate easily between groups numbering eight and twelve, for instance, a ratio of two to three. This takes a few more months to achieve. While these abilities may seem impressive, your infant is unable to say, let alone read or understand, the actual words "one," "two," or "three."

Your young baby's sensitivity to small numbers is astounding, because it shows the extent to which he is already processing the numerically relevant details of his environment. This ability will enable him to make quick assessments of changes that may occur around him: items rolling off the edge of his highchair, people leaving the room, one of his teddies missing from his crib, and so on.

He also uses quantification to track objects. So, for instance, at only a few months of age, if your baby sees two little trains disappear into a toy tunnel, he will expect both to come out the other side. Similarly, if two of your friends stop by for a visit and one leaves before the other, your little one will notice the absence without necessarily having watched the person exit the room nor having had the time to form a mental representation of what each person looked like.

By five to seven months of age, your baby's knowledge of small numbers has significantly developed, so that he will now be able to perform simple arithmetics. When you look at your small, babbling baby, this may seem hard to believe. Yet, amazingly, his brain is already capable of simple addition and subtraction. He will correctly realize that adding one plus one makes two, or subtracting two from three makes one (see the box on page 152).

An ingenious experiment was devised to investigate early mathematical abilities in the human infant. Placed in front of a little stage, five- to seven-month-old babies were shown a puppet display. A bear puppet appeared on the stage, and once it captured the infant's attention, a screen was lowered, concealing the bear from the baby's sight. A hand then appeared on stage alongside the screen, holding another bear puppet. As the infant watched, the hand containing the second bear disappeared behind the screen, then reemerged holding nothing (the implication being that the hand has left the second bear behind). The screen was then removed to reveal either one or two puppets. Amazingly, babies showed great surprise when only one puppet was left on stage. This surprise comes from the fact that the infants correctly assumed that when the second puppet was added to the first, this should have resulted in two bears on stage. The single bear was an unexpected outcome because 1+1 cannot equal 1.

Another similar experiment showed that babies know that 1+1 cannot equal 3. The hand added only one puppet, as before, but when the screen was raised, there were three bears instead of two. Again, babies showed surprise at this impossible outcome by looking much longer at the three. Their behavior indicates that they correctly expected to see more bears when the screen was lifted, and knew that it should be just one more bear, not two—an amazing feat for infants who were barely old enough to sit. To test infants' ability to subtract, three puppets were shown dancing on the stage. A screen then appeared concealing all the puppets and a hand visibly took one of the puppets away from behind the screen. However, when the screen was raised, there were still three puppets. Again, babies showed surprise at this outcome, demonstrating that even before your little is able to sit unsupported, he is already en route to becoming an accomplished little mathematician.

However, it isn't until language production is well under way that your toddler can clearly express his numerical knowledge to you. By this stage, you and others around him will be actively encouraging him to learn how to count by providing number words whenever relevant, and encouraging counting songs and rhymes that he will be encouraged to reproduce. You may find that your toddler initially uses an incorrect sequence of words when counting. For instance, he may count four objects by saying, "One, two, four, five." The words may be in the incorrect order, but if he uses them always in this order, then his counting system is governed by a clear logic based on a series of number-relevant principles (see the box, opposite).

Your toddler's personal sequence of count words will be only temporary, and he will rapidly come to conform to the conventions of his mother tongue. A toddler who uses the correct sequence from the start does not necessarily have a more advanced number system than one who counts using the wrong order, because sometimes correct sequences are learned by

The first principle governing a toddler's valid numerical system is one-to-one correspondence, whereby each number word, whether it is the correct term or not, refers to a different object in the sequence.

The second principle dictates that the words should always be used in the same order—so, in our example, your toddler would always use the word "four" to refer to the third item if you asked him to recount the same display several times without correcting him. The errors made by young talkers aren't really surprising, if you stop to consider that there is no logical reason why our language has chosen the particular syllable "two" to represent the number concept "2." The actual word is arbitrary and obviously differs from language to language.

The third principle is item indifference; any item can be called "two" in his counting system as long as it is the second one he counts. So in the example, your child has correctly understood that quantifying involves specific count words spoken in a fixed sequence; what he has yet to learn is how to recite the counting terms in the correct order. He must also learn what is known as cardinality. This is the principle that dictates that when you count a set of things, the last number represents the total number in the set. This is something that will take your toddler many more months to realize.

rote and recited more as a poem than as a method of counting. In fact, an 18 month old may be able to correctly recite all the numbers up to ten without knowing they have anything to do with numbers. Or he may use the labels "one, two, three, four" for only three objects, counting one of them twice. It is only when the sequence obeys the three principles in the box that you can be fairly certain your child is counting and the words are fulfilling a numerical purpose.

Learning to plan ahead

From early on, your baby shows an ability to solve simple problems by making plans. Problem solving in this way is not as straightforward as you might think. It involves generating a goal, finding ways of overcoming obstacles, using the resources available, and, finally, evaluating the outcome of one's behavior. So next time your baby succeeds in finding a desired object by turning over his toy box to rummage more easily through its contents, stop and reflect on the complexity of his ingenious behavior.

The first six months of life are a time when your baby gains a great deal of knowledge about how to influence and affect the things and people around him. As early as two months of age, he is able to work out basic problems, such as the need to kick a foot to produce music or make a colorful display move. By six months, he will discover which buttons produce which sounds and will be able to operate the right button to reproduce a sound he wants to hear. And by the end of his first year, your baby can hold a goal in mind long enough to first complete a subgoal . So, for instance, your one year old will deduce that he has to push one object aside to get at another, and he will do this without getting distracted by performing the subgoal (for instance, stopping to play with the obstructing toy). Interestingly, problem solving is considerably more successful when the task in hand is embedded in a meaningful context. So, your baby will come up with ways of finding a hidden toy more spontaneously in his own home environment than in the surroundings of an infant-testing laboratory.

Problem solving with trial and error

The earliest form of problem solving—used by an infant under six months—is what is known as "trial and error," something adults also use in new situations. It is the simplest way of seeking a solution and often emerges out of general exploration more than active planning. If your young baby wants to reach a toy, for example, he will try out all the possible strategies available to him to get hold of the toy—for instance, reaching out in different positions, crying out for help, or simply waiting—until by chance one of his strategies works. At this age, he is not able to judge in advance which one of his plans will more probably succeed. Although trial and error may be crude and unsophisticated, it does require that your infant keeps track of what he has already tried. Without this ability, he wouldn't necessarily progress from one strategy to the next and might end up reproducing the same unsuccessful attempts nonstop. Although trial and error sometimes occurs as a chance outcome of general play and exploration, the two activities are, in fact, not the same. Scientists found that, compared to when they are playing, babies' heart-rates decrease when they are actively problem solving, indicating a significant increase in the attention they are giving to the goal-oriented task.

"Forward search" problem solving

A somewhat more advanced form of problem solving involves "forward search." This is sometimes also known as "hill climbing" and entails using strategies that at each step bring your infant closer to his goal. Faced with a dilemma such as retrieving his ball from under the couch, your eighteen month old will need to think forward if he is to achieve his goal economically. This involves prioritizing the choices of strategies and props available for the task. Although at this age he may not yet be able to pinpoint the best option by predicting the outcomes of all possible actions, he will be able to avoid the strategies that he knows in advance won't help him reach his goal. So he will not attempt to squeeze his whole body under the couch, for instance, nor will he try to access the toy from the wrong end. He will instead probably try reaching from the nearest edges, and if that fails, he may work out that he needs to use another object to extend his reach. Alternatively, he may just give up and shout until you come to the rescue and retrieve the ball for him—a fail-safe strategy for the frustrated problem-solver who decides that doing it alone just isn't fun any more.

Use of means–end analysis

The most complex form of problem solving, called "means–end analysis," doesn't usually appear until after the first year. This is the ability to work backward from the desired outcome, via a series of subgoals, to find the most appropriate means to reach a goal. To do so, your toddler will have to assess what differentiates the current state from the desired state, and his chosen course of behavior must be aimed at reducing this difference. Although this is a relatively late development, your ten-month-old baby will already display the beginnings of this ability when he tugs on a cloth in order to bring a toy resting on it close enough to reach (see the box, below).

Taking all this on board, it is incredible to think just how far your baby progresses in his first two years: from those early triumphs of voice recognition and tracking, to learning that people have theories of mind and that the world of objects works according to rules; to being able to combine all the knowledge he has gained from his physical, cognitive, social, and emotional experiences; to making sense of the world, conquering the hurdles of daily life, and achieving a level of real independence.

MORE ABOUT **ASSESSING MEANS–END ANALYSIS**

One study examined this type of behavior across the developmental span between nine and 18 months of age. Infants were shown two cloths, the tips of which were within their reach. An exciting toy was placed on the far end of one of the cloths. Babies of all age groups immediately tried to reach the toy. Those under nine months pulled indiscriminately on both cloths. However, most infants between ten and 12 months of age grabbed only the cloth on which the toy was placed to pull it closer. They also knew not to pull on the cloth if the toy was placed beside instead of actually on top of it. Problem solving in babies is limited, however, because when three cloths were presented, only 18 month olds consistently pulled the right cloth. Younger babies seemed overwhelmed by the number of choices. They were no longer able to make a quick assessment of the situation and instead resorted to trial and error, pulling each cloth in turn until they were able to find the correct one.

By the latter half of the second year, children also display the capacity to understand the goals of others. In one study, for example, toddlers watched a video of an adult trying but failing to perform a number of target actions. They were never shown the successful outcomes. Yet, when presented with the same goals, toddlers did not copy the failed actions they had seen, but acted out the action the experimenter should have performed, given his goal. In other words, they do not just imitate blindly; they assess what the other person is trying to do, and copy his goal.

Coping with frustration

Young children tend to get particularly despondent when they are unable to achieve their goals. If you notice your child becoming increasingly baffled and annoyed by something, step in and gently encourage him to try again. Above all, show patience, and instead of simply solving the problem for him, help him to find an alternative strategy. Babies differ in their level of determination, patience, and strength of will. Some refuse to give up, no matter what the obstacles, while others are far more laid back and will simply move on to something else if a task isn't going the right way.

Problem solving is not just a matter of intelligence and maturity; it is inherently bound up with individual personality as well as outside influences, such as child-rearing practice. A child who is rarely left to his own devices and is used to having everything done for him at the slightest whimper will be less inclined to go through lengthy processes of trial and error. One study even noted differences between the sexe; at the age of one year, boys tend to cry less than girls when unable to attain their goals, but by twenty months, girls vocalize more for help from others and show less frustration than boys. In general, research has pinpointed the importance of secure bonding (see Chapter 2) in infants' attitudes to actively exploring their world and solving problems. Those who have established healthy parental attachments are more enthusiastic and less apprehensive about new situations. Mother–child interaction when trying to accomplish a difficult task is also more effective in children who are securely attached. This yet again highlights the role of emotional stability in intellectual development.

Learning through pretend play

As your toddler heads toward his third year, you will notice the onset of increasingly complex pretend play. This is an exciting milestone that occurs some time around eighteen months of age, when your baby no longer sees an object simply in terms of its functional use (a comb is for brushing hair), but begins to appreciate the potential symbolic meaning that an object can hold (a comb can be anything you want it to be, if you can suspend your knowledge for a while and give the object another meaning). This development enables children to invent instead of just imitate, a skill that is particularly salient to play.

Clearly, being able to pretend opens up new opportunities for fun. Yet, what does it tell us about intellectual development? Children play in many different ways: through imitation, by reenacting events that they took part in or witnessed, by making use of toys and tools, and by inventing new and imaginary scenarios. Unlike other forms of play, pretend-play involves the suspension of real-world knowledge and the introduction of make-believe. Take the following example: A young child picks up a banana and pretends to talk into it like a telephone. To play this game, the toddler has to set aside everything he knows about bananas—that they are yellow and soft inside, that they can be peeled and are eaten. For the period of time his little game lasts, he must temporarily replace all he knows about bananas with the things he knows about telephones—that they are rigid, have buttons and sometimes a wire, that they make noises, and let you speak to people who are not present. All this involves difficult mental gymnastics.

By placing reality on hold, the child achieves what is called "meta-representation" of the world. In other words, he manages to lift the internal image of the world that he has formed to a higher level, where it doesn't simply represent reality but can also take on an imaginary world. And he must do this while at the same time retaining all he knows to be really true about phones and bananas in his long-term memory.

Testing theories

Pretend play allows for children to manipulate the information they have stored in their memory to test out theories about the world, both physical and social. It can be elaborate, with complex events and situations being acted out and altered, and different roles enacted (teacher/pupil, cowboy and Indians, mommy and daddy, brothers and sisters). Children use this kind of symbolic play not only to broaden their exploration of the world but also to work out the rules of social interaction. Through play, they try out role reversal. For instance, what happens if baby tells off mommy for a change? Or if daddy asks baby for permission to eat chocolate cake? Such games can also provide your child with a stage upon which to revisit emotionally tricky situations, thus helping him to deal with difficult feelings he may experience.

Pretend play really comes into its own when imaginative make-believe is involved. It is the best platform for exploring the fabricated realities that make fairytales so enchanting—stories involving giants, aliens, talking animals, and magic. In this type of play, your child won't alter what he knows to be true through symbolism. Instead, he actually will invent a whole new reality for himself. This is a truly remarkable skill, because it shows an ability to use his imagination not only to transform but also to create new ideas.

Encourage your child

You should support your child's budding imagination by encouraging instead of discouraging pretend play. Never treat fantasies as untruths. Instead, do your best to engage and delight in your little one's flights of fancy. Childhood doesn't last long—before we know it, our children are grown and the early years are just a collection of memories and photographs.

So make the most of this time, when your child is learning new things every day and is still young enough to believe in true magic.

Index

Acknowledgments

Thank you to all the babies who helped with the photography for this project.

PICTURE CREDITS

Professor Stuart Cambell p. 12

Photolibrary.com
p. 14, pp. 20–21, p. 22, p. 23, p. 26, p. 28, p. 37, p. 40, p. 41, p. 43, p. 44, p. 45, p. 46, p. 47, pp. 52–53, p. 60, p. 68, p. 69 (bottom), p. 79, p. 82, p. 83, p. 84–85, p. 86, p. 89, p. 105, p. 112, p. 119, p. 139, p. 141, p. 143, p. 148

Getty Images
p. 27, p. 33, p. 69 (top), p. 99